The Beautifully Chaotic Life of Brandon Smith-Johnson

Brandon Smith-Johnson

ISBN: 978-1-8384686-7-5

i

Published By: -

i2i

PUBLISHING

i2i Publishing. Manchester.
www.i2ipublishing.co.uk

Contents Page

Acknowledgments..................................Page v

Chapter 1..Page 1

Chapter 2..Page 21

Chapter 3..Page 41

Chapter 4..Page 63

Chapter 5..Page 83

Chapter 6..Page 103

Chapter 7..Page 125

Chapter 8..Page 145

Chapter 9 ....Page 165

Chapter 10..Page 185

Acknowledgements

Rest In Peace Dad
You Are No Longer In Pain xxx
I Love You x
Until We Meet Again x

Thank you to everyone who has ever supported, loved and helped me in any way, shape or form. I am truly blessed for all the guidance and love given to me. Thank you to my wonderful family for everything you have done for me. I owe you all a piece of my heart. I love you all. xxx

Chapter 1

I was sixteen and in my final few months at Almondbury High School. That is when life started to change. I was picked on for being different and not conforming to everyone else's views. I wasn't popular with girls and didn't have a huge social circle, I wasn't one of the popular ones. I wasn't like anyone else, I was the individual one in the class and I saw things differently to others. I have always wanted to be the brightest star to shine amongst the night.

I always wanted to be known, seen and heard. I am gonna be successful! I desire it with all my heart, mind and soul. I have always felt so very different to the rest of society. A golden one is what I am. I am a golden soul, special and rare. I am gonna take good care of my family and my mother and also donate millions to charity. I have always, always dreamt of that happening, ever since I was about sixteen. I feel like I don't belong anywhere in this world, I have never felt a part of anything at all.

I don't gel with anyone or any place in this modern world, I feel like I was born in the wrong era. I feel like I don't fall into any category nowadays. I feel like a ghost wandering in the night, I am part of this world but on the other hand I am far away from it as can be. I have never felt connected to anything in this modern world, I don't even fully know myself, I feel like a wanderer of a different time, like I was dropped into this world at the wrong time and place. Oh, I truly feel like an alien amongst sheep.

Getting back to it though, school wasn't for me as I felt school didn't teach me anything of value besides my ABC's and 123's; basic knowledge is all we truly need to get started in life. Everything else that we use as knowledge is gained outside of the green schoolyard gates, I know about life just from living it. School can't teach life at all, only what you may use in college and university.

I remember being in Year 10 I think it was, it was snowing quite badly at school and at that time I was doing a photography class at another school with a few people from my high school year. As we were all waiting for the taxi to pick us up from school we started to all have a snowball fight and we went mental throwing ice bricks at each other! Well I had decided to pick up this block of ice and lob it at my friend who was stood in front of an ICT classroom window, behind which a full class was having a lesson.

I threw it at him but then he bloody ducked and it went over his head and through the window to land onto someone's computer keyboard. I remember looking through the hole in the window and staring at the guy whose keyboard it was and his face looked like he was caught in the act, I bet he was frozen in fear! Luckily enough I didn't get billed for the damage, I didn't mean to - it was purely driven by innocent fun.

I have always said that ever since I walked out of the school gates on my last day of high school, time has just blown away so very fast. In school I felt time dragged on quite a bit, I left at sixteen and it is like I blinked and I was eighteen, then I blinked again and now I am twenty-two going on twenty-three. I remember the innocence I had whilst being in school, I had nothing to worry about. No money problems of my own, not old enough to drive so that wasn't gonna cost me. I had my skateboard or bike to get around.

Being a kid ain't bad at all, school may have been boring and long but those days I had nothing to stress about. I love all my family so dearly, forgive me for my sins and my many mistakes. I appreciate you all! I remember when I had left school I had a sense of ultimate freedom and joy to do whatever I like, to enjoy not being

2

in the shackles of school and those long soul draining lessons. I never really fit in anywhere in society's social groups, I am not like anybody else I have met, it is like I am a chosen one or something.

I just see through all these people's masks and defensive ways that they use in life, I know a lot of people but I have no friends if I am honest. I have people I nod at in passing and people who wave or say hello when they see me out in the streets. Apart from that I don't have friends who I can call or text in the way of comfort and support. I remember having all these school mates and college friends that I used to knock about and smoke with and go to parties now and then with.

I remember being in college when I was around sixteen. I was studying Art and Design Level 1 at Kirklees College for about half a year until I was kicked out for threatening a guy in my class with an art scalpel. He had pushed me off my chair for no reason at all and tried to embarrass me in front of all the class. I wouldn't have used the scalpel at all, it was just a threat said out of instant anger caused from someone trying to humiliate me. All my life more or less I have always been someone who has had the piss taken out of them and was bullied and made fun of.

I have been called all kinds of names simply because I have dressed differently to others and done my own thing instead of following and becoming slaves to the views of others. I was born individually from everyone else so why am I gonna follow now? I hate sheep, I am an alien amongst sheep. I always will be separate from the rest, I am real. I never fitted in and never will fit in. I don't want to fit in at all. I shine too brightly to be hidden away and my bright shine shall never fade. I will live for all eternity.

I got kicked out and at that time me and my mother were living in Liversedge, I actually loved living there as it was surrounded by fields and hills for nice walks which I had gone on and smoked a joint or two in a field during the summer months. It was a wonderful time being eighteen until the point of meeting Lauren and then all of the shit that followed that girl soon hit me too. I was studying at Leeds City College doing my maths and English with functional skills too.

It wasn't bad at all being in Leeds, it was definitely a change of scenery and a much bigger place than Huddersfield. I enjoyed being at that college as I met all kinds of people from different places, countries and backgrounds. I remember smoking a cig in the smoking shelter outside of college. I saw this girl who looked foreign, she looked Mexican or of some Vietnamese decent. Coal black hair and dark eyes, tanned skin and a unique nose. She was smoking a cigarette, a sterling cigarette I was soon to find out, wearing a grey Nike jumper and jeans with a scowl on her face as though she found her prey and was ready to attack.

The girl I was staring at was my future girlfriend Lauren, oh that relationship was more toxic than nuclear radiation. She was a violently embarrassing drunk who had embarrassed me in basically every place we went and in front of every person we had met on nights out and on those drunken walkabouts we went on. On Leeds City streets with a bottle of Gordon's gin and in the backstreet bars with strangers we only just met.

It is annoying because I am such a charming guy and such a caring person that I get taken advantage of. I end up being pushed over and let down like a lead balloon at times. I have always been the chaser in talking to girls, always been the one to be showing more love than they do me. Always been the one to go further and help as much as I can whether that's giving people money, weed, food or clothes with no intention of getting something in return. I have always been a giver and always will be a giver for those less

4

fortunate than I. I know what it is like to be on my arse with nothing, not even a cig or a quid to hold in my hand. I have had to steal food to survive and ask people for cigs and rollups.

I hate asking for things, I have felt like a loser at times. I just want people to know that once I am completely successful in life, I will help those who have helped me. I will buy my mother a house and a car and take care of my family. I will give plenty to charity, even build and fund a psychiatric hospital. As I know myself that when I have been in a crisis and needed help there has been no beds available for me to stay in hospital so I want to give everyone an opportunity to get the help they need, regardless of their situation.

I remember the time I slept outside on the cold concrete and it was across from the police station in town, I had wrapped myself up in a foil blanket and used my backpack as a pillow. I rolled my last little pocket rocket to help ease my head into sleep. I had never in all my twenty-one years of living ever stayed outside before, only in a sleeping bag and a tent when me, Lauren and her family went camping at the Lake District on Lake Windermere back when I was twenty years old.

I had laid there against the cold brick walls with a roadworks barrier surrounding me. A big orange barrier with red and white glow-in-the-dark stickers. I was laying there thinking 'How could my life have possibly got like this? How the hell can I get out of this situation I was deeply in?' I remember living at my sister's when my mother and I had to sleep on the living room floor. We had to deal with it and go to sleep as there wasn't any room elsewhere in the house. Me and my mother had lived there for a couple of months, it was overcrowded as my nephew was in one room and my sister had her bedroom so the only place to sleep was the floor as the couches were far too small to sleep on.

Small, chocolate brown leather ones, two seaters that can't fit a person laying down on them. It was strange me sleeping on the floor next to my mother at the age of sixteen and still going to college every day too. I remember getting the 371 Dalton bus, I used to take that bus every morning to town to get me to college, I used to sit on the bus with an aching back and a bright vision of my success in the world. I started making art and doing photography at the age of sixteen. I started making collages and taking photos with a disposable camera, to then cut and paste the photos into notebooks and onto canvases with which I then painted an array of colours on to brighten the canvas.

I enjoyed college at Kirklees until I got booted out even though I didn't do anything. I used a verbal threat, the other guy pushed me off my chair. Of course one is going to be angry. I did a lot of artwork in Kirklees College as I used to take my sketchbooks home and create my own art with cut up dishcloths, cardboard boxes, canvases and paints, I used basically whatever I had at my sister's at that time. I still have two of my sketchbooks from when I was a teenager, they are seven years old. I have taken those sketchbooks everywhere with me that I have ever lived.

I have a collection of all my work; writings, art, photography pieces and a variety of my previous creations. All of it I hold so dearly to my heart as they hold the most sentimental of values in my life. I want to publish all of my work, every last piece of my work I want publishing and sharing with the world as I want to help millions of people with my pain and the suffering that I have endured throughout my life. So that they do not have to make the mistakes I have or if they have done already then they can view how I survived the harshness of life's times and how I coped in desperate times.

I have always had this truly deep and golden feeling of being successful through my pain and suffering, as through the suffering I mastered it into my art and writings. I truly crave that life, I deserve it. I just feel like from what I have endured in my life that it is all meant for something much, much bigger than what I could ever imagine. Like the universe's great masterplan for my life, I have many different styles and techniques, I am endless with talent and wonder. I am not like anybody else, I have always felt so differently to everyone I have met and spoken with.

I have always felt like I am a chosen one, like a golden soul that is here to be an inspiration and help to millions. I am special, I have always wanted to be famously successful ever since I was around sixteen or seventeen. I have always had this feeling within me that I was born to shine and live for all eternity. I have always had people in different ages and places tell me that I am gifted and that I will be a millionaire. I don't know why they said that but they must have seen something from the outside looking in, rather than me being on the inside and having trouble seeing what they are seeing.

I don't know but they can't all be wrong can they? They must know or have seen something in me. I have always felt so different to others, I have lived an experienced life and I am only twenty-two which makes me feel older as I have had to be more mature for my age in certain circumstances. I have always dreamt of having my own book published and being loved by millions through my gifts that the universe blessed me with. Living in a beautiful house, driving my favourite car and adoring my lovely wife.

Living content as a star that has made it. Knowing I made something of myself coming from nothing. I have always wanted that lifestyle, I deserve it as I have endured so much shit for one lifetime. I have struggled, pained, hurt and suffered so deeply and traumatically in my life that I do feel like I deserve to be a success. I have lived wildly and madly, seen and done many things of all descriptions. I have lived in many environments from abandoned care homes to addict riddled B&B's to lost youth hostels and troubled people hotels.

I have met people from all over the place with memories of their own that burn deep in pain, I have met heroin and crack addicts who have shot up and smoked in front of me, I have met young adults who have been in prison, I have met mentally unstable people who have demons that torment their everyday lives. I have met people who have had evil flowing within them, I have seen evil acts done to others and felt them done to myself.

I have been under the same roof as a rapist, I didn't know he was one, well me and Lauren didn't know he was one until that dark night in Leeds, I was eighteen and Lauren was nineteen. We had been drinking in the Angel Inn pub in Leeds town centre. I remember drinking in this pub one evening with Lauren and we had been doing coke, we drank some more until we were both past tipsy. We were both sitting down in the seating area inside the Angel Inn. We were drinking and joking when this guy who is a rapist comes over to me and Lauren and starts making conversation with us both, we were both pretty drunk by this point and quite coked up too.

So we were chatting to this guy out of pure intoxicated emotions and when you get drunk you become pretty talkative and confident so because of that we both didn't think anything of this guy. We just thought he was being a friendly pisshead who was also doing coke that night. He was with his friend and they were both pretty intoxicated themselves, come to think of it. It was like they were both partners in crime, like they used their tactics to find victims for their horribly

8

evil ways.

They act like they are your friend, buying alcohol and giving you coke to butter you up so that you warm to them, becoming under their control without knowing and then they can make their move. Both of them asked me and Lauren if we wanted to go back to their flat to a little gathering to drink and snort some more. As naive as we were, we both said "Yeah, of course, let's go!" We left the Angel Inn with smiles on our faces thinking that we were gonna have a wildly fun night as youngsters. Oh how wrong were we!

The four of us walked to the bus stop to catch the bus to the flat. We got on the bus and then we were on our way. We went to some location out of Leeds City centre, I had never been to Leeds much when I was eighteen, I had only recently started college there. We got off the bus then the rapist said that we had got off at the wrong stop. He said we had to walk to a different bus stop back to the right way to his friend's flat. I came to realise that he was planning a way of doing something to Lauren without me being there. That's why he had a friend to use as a distraction, he had told me and Lauren that we had to go separately on different buses.

Lauren went with him and I was to go with his friend on a different bus so that he could get Lauren on her own and attack her without me knowing, he made up the excuse that he had a bus ticket for two people and that only him and Lauren could go on one bus and I had to go with his friend on another using his friend's two person bus ticket also. It was all well put together, the way they both acted and spoke. Me and Lauren were on different buses going to the guy's flat, me and his friend got to Leeds bus station and waited round the corner by the market stalls.

I felt it was strange that Lauren and the other guy were nowhere to be seen. I started questioning the guy's friend and told him to ring his friend and ask where they are. He kept saying "Don't worry about it they are on their way." He gave me more coke and I smoked a cigarette as we waited for Lauren and his friend to come meet us. Eventually they turned up and we all walked from the bus station to the high-rise block of flats not too far from the city centre. We got to the flat and the house looked like a crack den, it was terribly unclean and there was a mattress and pillows in the living room.

It was badly decorated and looked like a hell hole, it wasn't a very homely place at all. It looked and felt more like a crackhead's house who didn't clean or have any morals to begin with, it was shocking. We all started drinking and doing more coke, the main guy had said he was off to the shop to get more alcohol. I think it was Three Hammers cider that we were drinking, disgusting stuff it is. He went to the shop and Lauren had gone with him, me and his friend waited at the flat, they were taking a while so again I started worrying and questioning.

I had messaged Lauren and she text me back saying that they were on the way back to the flat. She kept sending weirdly cryptic messages that made no sense, but I thought 'Maybe she's just coked up and pissed' as I was quite far gone myself. They got back to the flat and I felt a sense of evil within the room. I just started feeling really horrible, like there was an evil presence giving off bad vibrations. The night went on and all of us were completely mashed. I was sitting on the couch with Lauren, the rapist stood up and his friend sat across from me on the dirty mattress.

The music was playing loud, the drinks and coke passed round, the rapist had asked to have a word with Lauren outside of the room as it was proper loud in the living room due to his friend turning up the music louder and louder. I thought nothing about his friend turning up the music loud. I soon realised that the rapist's friend was using the music as a cover for what was going to be Lauren's screams for help. So I couldn't hear what was happening in the next room due to the loud music – these guys were messed up.

Looking back now, I know I should have realised sooner rather than later what was going on and that we both should have left as soon as it started becoming strange. Now I see the truth of the situation and what was really going on but back then I was high on drugs and alcohol, my mind was taken advantage of by two evil bastards. I was manipulated and deceived. I was young and naive, anyways before Lauren left the room she had written on her phone notes to then show me, the message said 'when I leave the room follow me two mins after, I am worried.' I discreetly nodded to her and then she left the room with him.

They went into the bedroom next door, I got up and told his friend that I was off to the loo but I was really checking on Lauren. I got outside the bedroom door and with my Doc Martens I nudged the door and there they were. Lauren was laid on her back with her top slightly up and my red, three inch braces I had lent her were down around her hips, the rapist was stood over her with this terribly scary look on his face. His Adidas joggers were partially down as though he was about to strike his sexual attack on Lauren.

Lauren looked lost and drowned in fear. He looked at me and I said "What is going on here, what the hell are you doing?" He didn't have one word to even say to me. It was like a deer in headlights moment, he threw on his dirt splattered yellow high-vis jacket, he used the jacket for his job as a warehouse operative. He got his Nike drawstring bag, then started calling a cab back to Halifax I think it was. He jetted out the front door, his friend was still sat in the next room wondering what the hell was going on.

Me and Lauren went back into the living room and

11

sort of sat there in total and ultimate shock. I started to smoke a cig and finish what drink I had left. Lauren kept asking me "Do you love me?" and saying "I am sorry." I was quite badly intoxicated in the exact moment but my brain and heart were both in disarray with pain. I went into the kitchen and started looking for a knife or something sharp so that I could mess these two guys up. I had found a blue screwdriver that was in a kitchen drawer, I was gonna stab both the rapist and his friend. He saw me with the screwdriver and fled out the door whilst still calling the cab.

Me and Lauren went to talk on the balcony about what the hell just happened, I began crying into my hands on the balcony as I still had the screwdriver in my jacket pocket. Lauren took it off me and said "He had forcefully touched my boobs and tried to take off my jeans." Luckily enough I had barged in on them in time. I had become cold and shut off after that moment as I was in so much shock and pain, I felt like I was powerless, I felt like I could have done more to prevent any sort of abuse but I had to deal with the situation in hand the best I could.

I had blamed myself for far too long after that night, the worst part of it was we had to stay the night in that flat knowing what had happened and knowing that we couldn't go anywhere till the next day as it was early hours and Lauren's house was locked and her parents were asleep and my mother was asleep thinking that her son is safe and well but I was far from it. We had no money for a taxi someplace else, we only had bus passes that college had given us. No buses were running as it was like 3:00 or 4:00 AM, it was so awful staying there that night.

We had drank some more and finished the coke we had left to sort of numb our pain for the night until we could properly talk and bleed our pain in our own time and place, we had stayed in the same room where

Lauren was abused which made my skin crawl and my mind go off on one. I was far from this planet in my head, so was Lauren, we were both really coked up and drunk, we both couldn't believe what had happened and why the hell we were still in this dirty, dark flat and how we got into this situation.

I wanted to ring the police but my hands were tied as Lauren said "No please, I don't want them involved, it will cause more hassle, I don't want my family knowing what went on." The next day came and we got up and left the flat ASAP, I remember Lauren saying to me as we were walking down the street, "Let us never talk about that night again and never go back to those flats again." We got back to Lauren's parents' house which at the time I was staying at, as I had left Liversedge where I was staying with my mother in a two-bedroom flat.

I left Liversedge to go live with Lauren but it wasn't that simple, I had packed my bag and left my mother's flat. I had met up with Lauren in Leeds city train station as Lauren had got a train from Bingley to Leeds to meet me. We went off and met up with a college friend. The three of us bought a bottle of Gordon's gin and a bottle of Sprite to mix it with. We used to knock about inside and round the back of the Corn Exchange building in Leeds, we used to get drunk a lot, in and out of college hours.

I remember we used to stay at my college friend's house a few times here and there, when we stayed at my college friends we would get drunk and take prescription drugs, I remember one time we all took a load of prescription meds worth hundreds that my college mate had got hold of. There were pills like codeine and other pain relief medications, we were drinking whilst taking prescription meds. Oh how stupid we were back then, we were young and idiotic I suppose.

I remember my college friend giving me one of his

father's flight jackets which his father had worn when he was a skinhead. His father sadly passed so he was left with his clothes. I always wore that flight jacket, I never did wear any other jacket but that. The jacket used to smell of gin, Sprite and cigarette smoke, it also was splashed with mud. This one time it was covered with blood as I remember having a razor blade in my wallet that I carried with me for some unknown reason.

Anyways the reason my flight jacket was covered in blood was because me, Lauren and some friends of ours from college were all sat in McDonald's in Leeds across from the indoor shopping centre, we were all intoxicated. I remember me daring my college friend that he wouldn't cut me with the razor, I don't know why I said that but he was drunk himself and he then decided to pick up the blade and slice the top of my left hand, I remember the skin just splitting and blood pissing out of my hand, I told him "What the hell did you do that for? I didn't think you'd actually do it." He laughed and said "Well you did dare me to do it, so I did it."

Oh the foolish shit I did as a teenager man. A few days passed and I remember me and Lauren sort of saying "What are we gonna do? Where are we gonna stay?" We couldn't go to our parent's houses as it wasn't allowed that I or Lauren have each other stay at our parent's homes. We had been out drinking with our college friend one night in Leeds when all three of us had no place to stay as it was late on in the night and we were all drunken messes, we had contemplated staying outside but said "Forget that, it's Goddam freezing man!"

We had walked around the streets of Leeds, the three of us had been drinking and I swear we had done coke that night too. We were quite destructive as a trio, we drank a lot and did drugs quite frequently. I think we were just three self-destructive, lost and bored teenagers who were rebels without any true cause. That night we

stumbled the streets and eventually cam
Leeds General Infirmary, we had decided as
place to go that we stay for the night in the waiti
of the hospital and sleep on the seats that were ou
the Costa Coffee shop.

I remember the drugs and drink hitting Lauren and she had asked me to get a paper cup so she could throw up. I handed her the coffee cup and she filled it within seconds, I sort of paused and thought 'What the hell is actually going on? Why am I sitting in a hospital waiting room, intoxicated and homeless?' I never thought that leaving home is like that, in fact it isn't for normal people but you gotta remember that I am not normal and neither was Lauren or anything in my life at that time so things sort of just happened.

Before I knew it I was staying in a homeless shelter with Lauren which was called The Crypt, The St. Johns Crypt I think it was called. We both stayed there for about three nights, it was another world living there. There were alcoholics, addicts and pretty much any sort of deeply troubled person who had an addiction or demons of some kind. It was foul living like that as there were communal showers and bedrooms. We had to sleep in separate rooms with like twenty other people, Lauren stayed in a room full of women and I stayed in another room with like fifteen other men.

Oh the smell was absolutely horrendous, it smelled of booze, cigarette, smoke, sweat, dirt and disease. I had never been in a place like that ever, I had never experienced anything of the sort before. I remember me and Lauren were sat outside the rooms we were gonna be staying in, Lauren was crying and pleading that she couldn't stay in the room without me there, I had comforted her, kissed her forehead and held her for a little bit until I persuaded her to go to sleep and that I would see her first thing in the morning.

The next morning came and me and all the other men

15

ff of the beds and place them
le of the room. I did that and
the next room so we could
fore breakfast, we met up
went outside for a cig. It was
so it was a pretty big shock
left our parent's homes and
nd safety we had got from
and we had to now fend for

...those three days before we were all off for Christmas for two weeks. We had left that day to go to college and as we got there we met up with our college mates. Me and Lauren had hung about after college with Zack and some other friends. We all got drunk and stumbled the streets of Leeds at night waiting to go back to The Crypt for our evening meal but we honestly wanted to stay out for as long as possible and get as drunk as possible so we didn't have to properly deal with our living arrangements.

We had got back later that evening to The Crypt so that we could get some food and chill out until we had to go to sleep, oh the drunken haze I had felt laying there in that foul smelling room with all those damaged beings. The night ended and the next day came and off to college we went, I think that we both left college early that day to sort out the next move of ours. Me and Lauren had gone back to The Crypt to speak with the staff there, they told us we had one night left to stay and that we had to leave and go to the council the next day to find a new place to go.

We were shitting it, we didn't know what the hell we were gonna do, we were only teenagers and had never lived outside of our parent's houses before. Me and Lauren went outside for a cig when someone who was living there had come up to us and spoke to us about finding a new place to stay, we thought 'Great let's go to

16

this new place then' ... bearing in mind that the guy who was showing us this place looked and sounded like Richard Ramirez. He had thick black hair, rotting teeth and an extremely gaunt figure.

He had come over to England from some other country, I can't really remember exactly where he was from but I do know he wasn't all there. I ain't calling him stupid but he really wasn't all there, he asked us to follow him to the new place we could stay, we walked through Leeds past the police station and crossed the roads towards the library and art gallery. We started to walk up the library steps and I thought 'This is strange, why are we heading towards the library?'

At that moment in time there was construction work being done to the library so there was scaffolding up and because of that there was a big fence that was surrounding the outside of the library doors. You could jump over it and sleep behind this big boxed fence and stay out of sight from society. We jumped over it and we looked at each other and thought 'No way in hell are we staying here.'

It was awful, to make matters worse Lauren had jumped over the fence her foot landed in shit. I don't know if it was human or animal but I know that no dog could have got over that fence as it was taller than me and I am around five foot eight. She had her Vans shoes on which she had got as an early Christmas gift. The Richard Ramirez looking guy was just pissing himself laughing at us both, it was probably his shit because how would he know that the spot was there and that there was this huge box fence to stay behind?

We told him "It is fine we will look elsewhere." It was a bloody weird time in both our lives, we were homeless and 'in love'. Love makes you do foolish things that you probably wouldn't have done otherwise. Me and Lauren had one night left to stay at The Crypt so we were a bit nervous as to what we should do next. The day caught

17

on and we went to the council in Leeds to find a property or at least try. We got into the housing place and they had basically told us because we aren't citizens of Leeds we couldn't be housed there. They gave us both a coach ticket to share to get us back to Huddersfield housing so that we could try in my hometown instead.

We left the housing place, went back into the town centre to walk and talk about what to do next, we sat on a bench and shared a cigarette. I had an IPhone 5 at the time, me and Lauren had no money for cigarettes or food as we had just finished our last one and were starving. I had decided to sell my phone at CEX so that we both could eat and get supplies to last us until we next had some money. I had got about eighty pounds for the phone which was quite good considering it wasn't in the best of condition.

I got the money and off we went to the shop to buy fags and food, then after we bought alcohol which was most likely Gordon's gin or white wine which Lauren was a slave for. She drank so much damn white wine, she was a full blown pisshead. We had bought a takeaway, a massive takeaway with loads of chips, burgers and wraps, we hadn't eaten properly in days as the food at The Crypt was only available in the morning and at night. We scoffed what we could and left to head back to The Crypt.

We got back and outside there was a group of people who were also living there. There was a youngish lad who seemed decent and he had started to ask me and Lauren about why we were there and what we were gonna do next. He volunteered there and had stayed there previously. He had asked us if we wanted to go with him and his friends, who were also staying at The Crypt, to go and smoke a joint and chill for a bit. We both agreed and off we went to get stoned, we had to walk to Chapeltown to go pick up the bud, it was a chill walk though.

We got to Chapeltown and we sat in some park and all of us passed round a joint and had a laugh and a chat. It was probably the most normal thing I had done that week. We had then walked back to The Crypt and gone and watched TV in the TV lounge. It was quite calm and relaxing to watch a film, well I suppose the reason I was so relaxed and unfazed by anything was simply because I was stoned. Plus I had my girlfriend beside me who was also high and drunk.

We were watching a film with the other people staying there. They too were high on something. They were defo smoking spice and drinking cheap cider. They were proper out of it, almost like zombies amongst the living. Quite scary how badly they were affected but also quite sad to see them destroy themselves. They were all pretty spaced out on something which I suppose at times helps the staff with their jobs as they wouldn't have to bother with such erratic people. I mean don't get me wrong there were still the odd mad people going off on one.

I remember this one time in The Crypt, this guy had gone into the toilets to do heroin and I heard from him that he was gonna kill himself. He muttered it to himself and I instantly felt I had to do something to stop him. I ran to staff quickly and told them. They luckily went into the loo and stopped whatever he was doing or gonna do just at the right time before he did something stupid. I had never been around drugs like crack or heroin before until I went into hostels, hotels and B&B's.

I have done many drugs but I am not proud of it all, I have had my times of despair and pain so I used substances as a coping mechanism in those horribly depressing times. This one time I was tripping and seeing all kinds of crazy nightmarish things, I saw demons with jet black bodies and red eyes, it had messed with my head. I was in some woods a long time ago when I was experiencing all of this, I was going in and out of a trip and my head was absolutely mangled, I was not in Huddersfield that night, I was in another dimension.

I lost one of my shoes and then found it again in the middle of these woods. There were loads of other people there too. They were all doing drugs and drinking madly. There was music till early hours and there was a massive campfire too. Towards the end of the party people had begun getting cold, so I decided to throw my cardigan on the dying flame and then all of a sudden the flame reached like eight foot above all of our heads. It was already a huge fire but I had wanted to make it bigger.

I was on a cocktail of drugs and loads of alcohol, I didn't care and I didn't know what on earth was happening. I remember these young chavs who came to the party in the woods, the reason they knew about the party is because the location was shared to the wrong group on Facebook. All these idiots decided to try trash the place and cause shit. They had punched this guy a few times and as they were leaving they smashed somebody's car window at the passenger side.

It was such a wild night that made me feel like a depressed corpse the following days. My comedown from that night was absolutely horrendous, I felt so suicidal and wrecked in all kinds of ways.

Chapter 2

Getting back to it though, I had never been around strong drugs such as crack or heroin until I was about nineteen when I was living in a B&B in Wibsey in Bradford. The final night at The Crypt was drawing to an end and in a couple of days it was gonna be Christmas 2016 and then it was going on New Year's so we had to find some place fast.

Even if it was a college friend's or a family member's house. We went to bed that final night with a hazy mind and drunken body filled with an array of intoxicants. The next mornin' arose and we got our bags packed and ready for the day ahead, we had got our breakfasts which included a nice hot brew, coffee to be precise. We had toast with our brews and then we said goodbye to the people at The Crypt. Oh we were glad to leave but felt a little sad to go as we had met some truly nice people who unfortunately had mad issues.

We had then walked into the city centre to make our next move, we had stopped outside the bus station, planning to use our coach ticket to get to Huddersfield. I said to Lauren "We could go to my dad's house and stay there for Christmas?" We had taken a shot in the dark and decided to go to Huddersfield and try stay at my dad's house, bearing in mind up until that point I hadn't seen my dad in years. Anyways we got to Huddersfield and then jumped on the Dalton bus to my dad's house, we got there and to be honest I was nervous as I didn't know what he was gonna say or do. I knocked on the door and my grandad answered.

Here I was tired, hungover, hungry and in need of a good shower and a sleep. My grandad greeted me and Lauren and asked us to come in for a brew and a sit down. My dad was upstairs getting changed when me and Lauren came into the living room. I introduced Lauren to my grandad and explained the situation, I was

21

glad to be around family and in a safer environment than the cold streets of Leeds and around the lost souls of its homeless community.

Again I ain't calling anyone out but I was much more settled knowing I was around family now and that I could finally have a shower and a decent meal. My dad came downstairs and I introduced him to Lauren also. He was happy to see me and I was him, he had asked me "What has been going on and what is your plan?" I told him "I don't have one, I have left home, I have been living in Leeds with Lauren. We are both homeless and need a place to stay for the time being."

He told me "I will speak to your grandad about it and let you know." Luckily enough we were both allowed to stay for Christmas, I was relieved. My dad had also given me some money for Christmas as he hadn't been around for years and then he took me to the shop to buy some cigarettes and alcohol. I had bought a bottle of Tennessee Honey Jack Daniel's and I had got Lauren two bottles of white wine. I had begun drinking from that day all the way up till the day me and Lauren were kicked out of my dad's.

I think it was about two weeks I had been drinking for. It was a messy two weeks, Christmas that year was strange. We had both got settled in and had a shower each and chilled out for the rest of the day. The next day came and my dad had offered us a lift to town to do some food shopping, we had gone to the Sainsbury's in Huddersfield town. Me, Lauren and my dad were walking around Sainsbury's when we bumped into my mother and my sister. They were so shocked and upset that me and Lauren were staying at my dad's as my mother and my dad were not together anymore.

My mother's face filled with anger and disappointment as I know she sadly felt betrayed by me. I didn't mean any pain intentionally to be caused, I was just young and 'in love', I didn't want any trouble to erupt but it did. My mother had shouted and screamed at me and Lauren with the reason being that Lauren had come over to my mother's flat in Liversedge in the early days of the relationship. Before we both left home, Lauren came over in like the first week of our relationship and brought white wine with her.

My mother was working late that night so the flat was free for me and Lauren. We drank both bottles of the piss smelling white wine, God I hate white wine! We got drunk and slept together. I had never had a proper girlfriend before either so I guess I became pretty enthralled pretty damn fast. I left the flat with her and then we got on the bus outside of Don Luigi's in Liversedge. It used to be called Don Luigi's, it may have changed now as it was over five years ago since all of this occurred.

Anyway we got on the bus to Leeds to then get Lauren on her Bradford bus. The journey was a long one but I didn't mind it as I had my headphones to use, I spent most of those bus journeys staring at life and the scenery around me. We got to Leeds bus station, Lauren got on her bus home and I waited for mine back at Liversedge, I loved the night time bus rides, the buses were usually quiet so I could relax a lot more. I got home and my mother was home also, she had begun arguing with me as she had found the empty wine bottles and was going on about drinking and what it does to people and all of that.

Another time Lauren had come to my mother's flat, she slept over and was on her period which caused her to bleed on my mattress. My mother at this point already didn't like Lauren for the wine bottles reason and the fact that she saw evil in her eyes. I mean mother is never wrong is she? Lauren had these dark eyes that looked as though she had a demon inside her soul, really scary eyes at times. My mother had found the bloodstains as I had stripped the bedding off and tried to clean the blood off the mattress.

She took major offence to the whole situation and decided to not allow Lauren back again. I told Lauren that she wasn't allowed back and I felt a huge blow to the relationship as I wanted to be able to bring her back home now and then to stay over. My mother had her reasons for not liking Lauren at this point but I was still 'in love' with her so I had decided to stay with her. Anyways going back to that day in Sainsbury's with Lauren, me and my dad.

My mother was angry at me for talking to my dad and for leaving home to live with Lauren, by this point my mother hated Lauren as I guess she saw it as her youngest child had been taken away from her and is now drinking heavily and doing all kinds of daft shit. I was no angel but I never in my life intended harm purposefully to anyone, I was just stupid, young and under the influence of pain and drugs. My mother had thrown her shopping basket down and it hit my foot, I was in total awe as I didn't know what to do or what to say to make the situation better.

My dad had sort of looked at me with a puzzled look as if to say "What the hell have they done for it to be like this?" We had stood there for a little bit feeling and looking embarrassed in front of this small audience of customers, I felt so embarrassed it was untrue. We had finished shopping and then returned to my dad's house. My oldest half-brother, who is my dad's other son, was sitting in the living room. I hadn't seen him in years and I still don't talk to him now.

I have never really had a relationship with my oldest brother. He was sitting in the living room at my dad's speaking with our grandad, he greeted me and Lauren and I introduced her to him. As it was Christmas time we saw a lot of my family who were coming round to my dad's. It was nice to see family from all over the country and world, I had spoken with my oldest

24

brother and had a catchup. I had a little bit of my Jack Daniel's whiskey and Lauren had some of her white wine.

We had heard from my grandad that my cousin was having a little Christmas do and there was going to be food, drink and music. Lauren and I were asked to go round and see my other family members. So that is what we did. We spent the rest of that day drinking and stuffing our faces with chocolates, ice cream and savory snacks. It was Christmas I suppose, the days passed and then it was the night of my cousin's little party. Me and Lauren had a shower and got ourselves dressed up for it.

We were raring to go and have some fun. My cousin's house was not that far from my dad's house, I reckon it was about a five minute walk. Anyways we had finished getting ready and made our way round to my cousins. Me and Lauren had arrived at the house and were greeted by my cousin, she had never met Lauren before so it was all a new interaction. The night started off at a slow, steady pace then as the night lingered on, it got quite eventful.

I remember meeting a family friend, my family on my dad's side are Jamaican/British and the family on my mother's side are Romany gypsy/British descent. I am still wanting to find out my full heritage properly as I know that I am not fully British, I am mixed race but I do not know my exact bloodline. Getting back to it though, this family friend had been using a pair of crutches to support his bad leg. I noticed he was quite stoned, I kept seeing him going out into the dryer room in the outhouse.

I thought 'This man is definitely smoking something' so I followed him but in a discreet manner. I got an instant nose tickle of weed. I thought to myself 'I wanna try some of his spliff.' I had followed him from the dining room where my cousin and her partner were making some Christmas food. It was basically an early Christmas dinner but with loads of Cîroc, wine, whiskey, beer and pretty much a whole brewery on tap for us all to enjoy. Jamaicans sure do love a drink, I had been drinking Cîroc mango neat. I thought 'Yeah man I can handle this, give me another one.' How bloody wrong was I.

I got into the outhouse where the family friend was and he was lent up against the dryer. He was turned facing the door as I walked in. I am pretty sure he knew what I was there for! I had sat down on this crate, I think it was a crate of lager, as there were no spaces elsewhere. I started to make conversation with the family friend, I had seen he was smoking a spliff. I anxiously asked "Please could I take a few burns?" How foolish was I. Oh wow!

Before he had passed me the spliff, in a slurred, drunken and very stoned voice he said to me "This ain't no normal bud this, this stuff is what we smoke in Jamaica." Bearing in mind I had been drinking before smoking which we all know the saying goes 'Bud before beer, you're in the clear, beer before bud you're in the mud.' Friggin' hell man, I was in the bloody mud alright, I had taken a deep three to four burns of this pure joint and instantly I knew I was disorientated.

I tried standing up from the crate and I fell right back down onto my arse again. It was like the weed had wrapped a skipping rope round my legs and had a firm grip of my brain so I couldn't walk or think anymore. I have no idea what kind of bud I smoked but what I do know is, is that he was right. It wasn't like no normal weed I had smoked before. I have smoked quite a lot of weed in my time, no I ain't boasting or proud of my previous substance misuse.

Whether that be drugs or alcohol, I have been so stupid with alcohol and drugs but I never was one to go out there and buy unreal amounts of whatever substance was available. I did them socially, I have not been 'addicted' to other drugs as much as I have been to weed though. I prefer to smoke weed than drink and I prefer to drink on occasion than take drugs on occasion. I have had my fun with drugs and alcohol for one life thank you!

I have done a lot of daft shit in my young years but I have never been one to cause trouble for others intentionally and with an evil mind. It has always been trouble and torment following me, not me looking for it. I have always been the person to try to avoid trouble of any kind, I am not an evil guy in any way, shape or form. I have always been the one to try and help as much as I can or I have been the one to advise and help others. I am great at giving advice but not that great at listening to it, whether it is my own advice or somebody else's.

It's like I have two brains instead of one, one brain says do something and the other one is finding every excuse not to do it. I have battles internally with myself at times, I struggle at certain points to understand myself and why I feel the way I do at times. I have a strong sense of isolation, I feel I do not belong anywhere as such. I am just a wanderer of life. I gather knowledge in the forms of pain, euphoria and much friggin' more. I have been on some crazily weird journey these last couple of years, as you know from reading all of this. I have much more to say so stay tuned in and see if you can find yourself within my words.

So getting back to it... I was on a 'whitey' which basically means I had begun feeling as though I was dying violently. Sweating, then going cold, then hot, then throwing up, then looking like a ghost and then your mind is frazzled with disorientation. I felt like I was dead basically, I had left the outhouse and jetted to the loo. All that friggin' Cîroc mango and Christmas dinner was soon to be in the toilet, as well as my face. I

27

couldn't stop throwing up, it was like I was getting hotter whilst having cold sweats.

I was defo on a 'whitey', Lauren was beside me as I was regretting everything that night. With my head in the loo and bloodshot eyes, I had finally stopped throwing up. I had walked down my cousin's stairs to the dining room, I knew that she knew I was high and on a 'whitey.' She had asked Lauren to take me back to my dad's house and get some sleep and a glass or ten of water. By this time my dad and his new girlfriend were in some fancy hotel someplace out of Huddersfield.

Me and Lauren stumbled up the street and round the corner to my dad's place. My grandad was home, he was asleep on the couch. Me and Lauren got inside and I ran so fast upstairs to the loo, at this point I am pretty sure there were no more fluids in my body. I felt as though a brick had hit my head at full pelt. I was clung to the toilet with my hands around the seat and my head leaning into the bowl. Lauren was just pissing herself laughing at me and then I had finally stopped dying.

I crawled into the bedroom where we were both staying, there was a huge king size bed and lots of pillows so I could lay in pure comfort. The night came to a close and into bed we got. Eyes shut and asleep, the room was spinning at like two hundred miles per hour though. Felt like I was in a wheel going down the M62 without breaks. The next day arrived and I had been lying in bed hungover with a blank mind as to what the hell happened last night.

The beautifully aromatic scent of fried egg and bacon danced up the stairs and into my nostrils. It was a lovely way to wake up after having such an eventful night. I put on my grey, winter style dressing gown and my slippers and down the stairs me and Lauren went. My grandad was cooking some breakfast of his own and said to me I could make something for Lauren and myself. I had cracked some eggs into the frying pan with some strips of smoked bacon.

I loaded the toaster with brown bread and waited for the bacon and eggs to be cooked to my liking. I had laid out the golden brown toast on two plates, I had spread the eggs onto both slices of toast then placed the smoky fried bacon on top of the eggs. It was like a lovely little bed of food, I then pulled out the West Indies hot sauce. This hot sauce is by far my favourite sauce as growing up I remember going round to my dad's for the night every Saturday. He would wake me up to a perfectly made English breakfast with a cup of coffee.

That West Indies hot sauce is what my dad used to use to put on my breakfasts. That is why many years later I still use it, I am addicted to it. I remember once as a kid I had tried opening a bottle of hot sauce and it had slipped out of my hand and hit the kitchen floor at my mother's house. The bottle broke and up into my eye came flying a drop of napalm-like hot sauce. Directly into my eye! Oh wow, I screamed like a girl! The hot sauce felt as though lava had been released into my eye.

My mother had told me to put my eye under the tap and wash the sauce out, I thought I was blind for life. I was only like nine or ten, being a kid is fun and free until you reach eighteen and you are in the open world. So jumping back to the morning at my dad's, me and Lauren had demolished our bacon, eggs and toast, then finished off our coffee with a Sterling Superking cigarette. We sat outside in the garden, the air was crisp and cool, I remember seeing the frost collecting around the window frames and the particles of ice that stuck to the grass which made it look like glass scattered upon the ground.

Oh wintertime is lovely when you are viewing the landscapes from indoors or you are having a quick cig at the back door or even a stroll out and about. Not so lovely when you are out doing errands with no proper boots or clothing. We finished our cigarettes and inside we went, we had spent a few days sort of just lounging about and doing nothing. It was the Christmas holidays after all, the next few days danced on and Christmas was here.

We had both got presents from our parents, Lauren's dad had dropped her's off. I got a dressing gown, aftershave, chocolates and a few other little gifts from my mother. My dad had given me money at the start of the holidays when we first went round. I did feel bad that I wasn't spending Christmas with my mother as I knew she was living on her own. At the time she was out of Huddersfield in Liversedge so she wasn't near family as such. I do feel like a bastard for how I have treated my mother and my family, I never meant to hurt anyone intentionally.

Like I said I was young and foolish, I was under the influences of drugs, alcohol and so called love. I don't blame anyone but myself of course! I have made many stupid mistakes, too many to count. The days had passed and my dad and his girlfriend had returned back to Huddersfield. My dad came round after being at his girlfriend's house to wish me, Lauren and his father a merry Christmas. We sat in the living room chatted for a while and opened the remaining Christmas gifts.

The drinks then started to flow for us all, I was down to my final bit of the Jack Daniel's Tennessee Honey and Lauren was on her last bottle of white wine. My dad had mentioned to us both that another cousin was having a little gathering. We were all going round later to see some more of the family. I was chuffed to be able to see other family members as at this point I hadn't seen anyone from my dad's side in a few years. I have a big family but I only see my mother, sister and brother nowadays.

I also see my brother-in-law and my sister-in-law

occasionally too. I don't really speak to anyone besides them if I am honest. I speak to my mother more than anyone else in my life. I do not have friends as I have never had true mates. Always people who either smoke weed, drink or do drugs. I have not had that one friend to sort of vent to, to let out my pain and have them listen carefully. I have always been a loner in some form or another. I have only had one proper girlfriend which was Lauren and then she ended up bloody cheating on me with my next door neighbour.

It was a long two years after that Christmas at my dad's that she cheated on me, she was my first proper girlfriend as well. Bitch had messed everything up that we had built throughout our relationship, I had always done my best with her. I had always tried, given and cared as much as I could but she never appreciated me ever. The worst part is, is that she truly feels remorseless. Oh well it doesn't hurt me no more, it just hurts to not be able to trust people, especially girls properly again. I am terribly afraid of getting close to anybody in case I experience a lack of loyalty again.

Maybe one day I might change and be able to trust that future angel of mine. Wherever she is, anyways to the night of my other cousin's gathering. Me, Lauren and my dad all started to get ready for the gathering and I remember Lauren having bleach blonde hair and postbox red lipstick on. She looked oriental, in that moment I had looked at her and thought 'Oh wow, I am so lucky to have her' but little did I know that she didn't feel the same deep down. I was another one of her tortured mental and emotional victims.

She didn't have emotions like 'normal people', she was something like a sociopath. She had many different layers to her false personas. I had hopelessly fell for a sociopath, she had this way of getting deep within my mind and heart and sort of starting wars within me that I didn't know were there. It had just taken Lauren to start it all off as she was the one holding my heart and mind in both her hands. As though she was holding that green putty stuff that if dropped will collect dirt, hair and any sort of bits that are on the floor.

My heart and mind were the putty and all the pain I had endured from her was the dirt, fluff and hair that collected upon my heart and my mind. I was trapped in an awfully toxic and abusive relationship. At first you have no idea what your 'lover' will put you through until it is too late and you are too deep inside the chaos. I had foolishly fallen into her Venus flytrap of a life. Me, Lauren and my dad had left the house, then we started to walk to my cousin's gathering.

It was a terribly cold night in December, I remember feeling the frosty air hit my face and my chapped lips. I was wearing my Harrington jacket, black jeans and Puma suede shoes. I hadn't many clothes as I only had what I carried in my backpack around Leeds when me and Lauren were staying at The Crypt. Me, Lauren and my dad had arrived at my cousin's house. We were greeted by one of my cousins, she was glad to see me after so long and I had introduced Lauren to her.

We entered the house and I saw my oldest cousin with his girlfriend and his kids in the living room. They were also very happy to see me. I had said my hello's and how are you's to everyone in the house. I was a bit peckish so I walked into the dining room and there it was. A lovely array of Jamaican style food, there were saltfish, dumplings, rice and peas, chicken, sandwiches and all other kinds of foods. I grabbed my white paper plate and I tucked in on some authentic Jamaican food.

I had mingled a bit with the family, Lauren was talking to my cousins and my other family members. It was nice to see everyone happy and together, I hadn't been used to spending Christmas like that before, it was always me, my mother, brother and sister that spent Christmas as a family. Up until this point where I was staying with my dad I had not seen or spoke to him in many years as my mother and my dad had split up years ago and never spoke again.

A lot of my battles I have fought on my own as nobody else could've fought them for me. Those deep, dark and most awful battles I have fought on my own. Only me and my twisted demons have battled. Nobody else has been there in those soul destroying moments but me, all those horrendous wars I have been there alone. I haven't had anyone to feel the pain as much as I have in those moments of despair.

The worst moments throughout my life, I have been the only one to see and feel the tremendous hurting and sorrow-filled events that have occurred within life. Yes my mother and my dad have both helped, cared and taught me a lot but I have won most battles alone. I feel so bad because I have not been the kindest to my mother or my dad previously. Again, I didn't mean to hurt anyone intentionally, I have just been battling demons of my own and took my pain out on her and the family.

We spent the remainder of the time at the gathering just sat talking to my relatives and having a few drinks with them. The night was getting on so me, Lauren, my dad and my dad's girlfriend left my cousin's place and walked back round to my dad's to check in on my grandad and drop some things off. We were all in the living room chatting and having a drink or two. We didn't know what our plan was as it was New Year's Eve the next night.

Me and Lauren had been asked by my dad's girlfriend if we wanted to come round and spend the rest of the night there to have a few drinks and listen to some music and mingle some more. We set off from my dad's house to his girlfriend's and on the way there his girlfriend had pulled out a pack of Chinese cigarettes that looked like thin cigars. They were quite strange tasting and seemed to last forever. I had finished smoking the cig before entering the house. She has a Japanese Akita which is white and grey, it looked like a bear. It was huge!

We took our shoes off and walked through the hallway to the kitchen. She asked if we wanted something to drink, me and Lauren agreed, then we sat around the kitchen table and began to sip our drinks. I remember seeing my dad's girlfriends' daughter and her boyfriend who were sitting around the table with red drinking cups. Her daughter's boyfriend looked pretty drunk himself. I said "Hello how are you?" and introduced Lauren to him. We were all now at the table and pretty tipsy.

Her daughter's boyfriend had begun telling us about an event in which he was involved in. He had told us all that he was driving around Dalton when all of a sudden somebody shot at him from the middle of the road. Luckily the bullet missed his head otherwise it would have killed him instantly. It was a case of mistaken identity and he wasn't the target, probably to do with drugs or gang activity. He showed us a photo of the bullet hole and it was in the middle of the windscreen, just below the rearview mirror.

How damn lucky was that? He could have died that night and through something that wasn't even his business. I bet he was counting his lucky stars that night. He had laughed off the whole situation but I know deep down he was shitting it. The night caught on and was soon to be over, the drinks flowed and our balances showed that. Me and Lauren had finished our drinks and got ready to leave to go back to my dad's place. I remember it being like two in the morning and feeling the icy weather that enveloped the streets of Dalton.

We stumbled back to my dad's, we got upstairs and we got into bed. I remember taking a shot of whiskey and resting my head on the pillow next to Lauren's. I fell instantly asleep with the help of the whiskey to ease my body into a gentle kip. It was the next day which meant it was New Year's Eve and that meant even more food, drink and laughter was to arrive. I mean drinking was a big part of my life for so long due to having an alcoholic girlfriend that depended on white wine almost every day of our relationship.

I hated the stuff, it smelled like pissy water and it had the colour of it too. White wine that is. She bloody loved the stuff, I have been in too many domestics with her due to the obscene alcohol content in her bloodstream. She has spat on me, scratched me, bit me, slapped me and kicked me many damn times. One time she kicked me with high heels on and she had split the skin on the side of my jawline. She has punched me and thrown objects at me which included a glass ashtray that hit my head and knocked me to the ground.

I have had cups, chairs and bowls thrown at me, as well as a round, red plastic toy box that was full when she'd emptied it on my head and then proceeded to whack me a few times with it as I laid on Zack's living room floor. She opened a pasta sauce jar that was full and then thrown it all around my bedroom at a hostel I was staying in, back when I lived in Bradford when I was nineteen. Then she'd thrown it against the wall into a million shards of tomato sauce-covered glass that were soon scattered across my badly stained and cig burnt carpet.

She once hit me round the head repeatedly with a kettle until it disintegrated into a thousand pieces.
She also at one point grabbed a kitchen knife from the draw in my mother's flat back in Liversedge where we were both staying. She had grabbed the kitchen knife but luckily it was as blunt as a butter knife. She had begun moving the blade slowly in a cutting motion on my left leg. Muttering to me "Why aren't you bleeding, why isn't it cutting you?"

Then she came out with the most messed up thing I

had ever heard which was "Let's go kill someone, we can wrap them up in a plastic sheet and bury them." I honestly hands down at this point thought it was all a big, sick joke and that she was just trying to scare me. She had always said some messed up things to me throughout our relationship, I knew that this girl was damaged beyond repair. She had evil in her soul and her eyes were dark and everlasting like the abyss. I was 'in love' with a psycho-sociopath, I was the abused and she was the abuser.

Now you may think 'Why on earth would he stay with her, why would he put up with that for two plus years?' Well it's like that when you're 'in love', it wasn't love really, it was a bad habit and a mindless infatuation. I didn't wanna be on my own again so I stuck with her to not fall back into darkened loneliness. I was so wrapped up with that girl that everything she did wrong I had to defend and be in her corner. She did have a huge damn hold over me from what she had done to my heart and mind over the space of two years. It started slowly, then gradually it got worse and worse until there was no easy return. I was hooked on her evil 'love' like an addict to heroin.

So going back to New Year's Eve... I awoke in the morning and I was ready to take on the day. I was majorly hungover as the night before at my dad's girlfriends' house I was drinking Captain Morgan's, Cîroc and any other spirit that was available for my liver to sponge up like a dishcloth. I guess Lauren's influences had clearly rubbed off onto me, I had never been a big drinker before I met her. I had just smoked weed, I know I was weak minded and easily led at times. I suppose I felt as though I needed to do certain things to fit in.

I have never been a part of anything that I can truly call my own. I have never had my own friends, I have never had girls chasing me and I have not been 'socially normal.' I was an outcast, an alien, a misfit! I have not one number in my phone contacts that I can call to vent or to just chat and talk about my pain and my troubled soul. I have felt as though I had been cursed in many ways. I have never been at war with anyone as much as I have with myself. Dreaming of holding someone close to me, my heart and my mind.

Enough of my pitiful words. Back to New Year's Eve, me and Lauren got showered, dressed and had our morning brew and cigarette. We had both been asked by my dad and his girlfriend if we wanted to go back up there again for New Year's Eve until the early hours of New Year's Day to count down to a new year and have some drinks and snacks. I believe that a new year is a clear out from the year before. We agreed to go to my dad's girlfriends' for New Year's Eve and count down into the New Year.

We didn't do much that day apart from chill out and drink some more. I know we went to town for an hour or so during the day, Lauren had got her nails done in a flamingo pink colour, long as hell and as sharp as razors. I had wandered off to buy myself some new clothes. Instead I got a white bucket hat from the money that my dad gave me due to him missing all my birthday's and calendar events throughout my life. I think it was like fifteen pounds for the hat, I only wore it a couple of times after that day.

I have a bad habit for buying things and either throwing them away, giving them to charity or destroying them in one of my many awful episodes. Lauren never wanted me to wear certain shit or do certain things as I guess this was one of her controlling methods in my life. We had finished off in town and got the bus back to my dad's house. We had made some food and poured ourselves a drink or three to get into the party mood. Time ticked on and the night was here for us to relish in, only a couple hours left until the New Year though.

We walked up to my dad's girlfriends' house and greeted them with smiles and positivity. Me, Lauren, my dad and his girlfriend all sat in the kitchen around the oak table. My dad's girlfriend had asked me "Do you want to have your hair cut?" as she is a hairdresser. I agreed to do so and then out came her special hairdressing scissors, they were sharp as hell. I grabbed a tea towel and wrapped it around my neck to stop the thorn like hairs pricking my back as they fell down my shirt.

I hate that, when I am getting my hair done and I end up walking round town like I have some sort of skin irritation going on. All due to the millions of hairs that fell down my top during a barbershop session. I was sat in the kitchen getting a trim and making myself look decent. Before Christmas I was stopping in The Crypt with Lauren and I had not properly slept, eaten or taken care of myself in a while so my looks had slipped a bit.

My dad's girlfriend had finished doing my hair, she had asked "Are you both hungry?" I pleaded "Yeah of course!" I adore food. She pulled out this packet of Chinese noodles, the noodles that I still to this day absolutely cherish as they are full of pure euphoric taste. I can't remember the exact name but the packaging isn't in English, they are something oriental sounding. I can't bloody remember, anyways these noodles come in a red packet with a Chinese meal pictured on the front and the font of the packet is black.

My dad's girlfriend began cooking the noodles and the smell was so friggin' gorgeous that I could have sold my soul for an unlimited supply of them. They weren't like anything I'd had before, these were special noodles. The noodles were finished cooking and into two ceramic bowls they went for me and Lauren to dig into. The noodles had a soup base and once the actual noodles were gone you could grab a slice of bread and dunk it into the delicious, flavour-filled soup. The soup was extremely spicy and full of euphoria that caressed my tastebuds.

Me and Lauren had scoffed the lot and returned to our alcoholic beverages. I was drinking rum and coke and Lauren... you guessed it! White bloody wine! Urgh! The night went on and we was all listening to some classic reggae by the names of Barrington Levy, Bob Marley, Eek-A-Mouse, Black Uhuru and many more names I simply can't remember due to the rum and coke having a nice, firm grip of my memory. The night went on and the conversations flowed, as well as the alcohol in my bloodstream.

I remember playing some cards with Lauren, my dad and his girlfriend. I had never really been into cards before so it was a new experience for me. It was coming up to the countdown to New Year's in roughly an hour or two's time so we all went into the living room to carry on the drinking and the conversations. It was weird as hell being around my dad and his new girlfriend because for so long I had grown up seeing him with my mother.

It was even weirder sat in his girlfriend's front room with him and my new girlfriend, all drinking and laughing together about to enter the new year together. It was the final hour of 2016 and we had all got ready for the countdown which we were watching on the television as every year in London they have the countdown and the fireworks which thousands gather for. We sat clung to our drinks, stuffing our faces with chocolate and a variety of finger foods.

It was coming up close to the countdown so we turned up the TV and watched as the minutes ticked by. I was pretty pissed at this point so I sort of just gazed into the TV with a drunken state and a grin on my face, ready and waiting for the countdown. Lauren was sitting beside me, my dad and his girlfriend were beside one another too. The countdown has started to roll,

"10! 9! 8! 7! 6! 5! 4! 3! 2! 1! HAPPY NEW YEAR!" We all cheered and chanted.

Chapter 3

It was now the new year of 2017, oh what new memories both wonderful and horrible would soon occur in that year. I could hear all the fireworks and cheers from around the neighbourhood that lingered in the air. Me and Lauren had decided to leave an hour or so later as it was knocking on quite late by the time we had finished our drinks and snacks. Me and Lauren had put on our jackets and shoes, by this point Lauren and I were pretty mashed up from the alcohol cocktail we had drunk throughout the night.

We said goodbye and wished a happy new year to my dad and his girlfriend, then closed the front door. I sparked a cig and we wandered down to my dad's place. Lauren was being way too damn loud and annoying to be walking around Dalton at that time in the morning. Now it isn't the area you want to be going around being noisy, pissing people off and causing shit. We had got outside my dad's place when Lauren, being the embarrassingly violent drunk she is, decided to lie on the ground.

She was being so bloody noisy to the point where people were shouting at us both from their bedroom windows. From the way it looked, I was stood over Lauren as she was drunkenly laid out on the ground. Her Vans shoes off her feet and in the road, it was like trying to stand up a dead person. She was paralytic and being violent towards me by hitting me and pulling my hair. This is what I had to deal with every damn time we drank together. She kept blurting out insults and being a massive bitch, I don't get why she had started being like this directly outside the place we were going into.

Not up the street nor down the street, exactly outside where we should be going in. The neighbours began to curtain twitch and I remember someone shouting "Oi what the hell are you doing?" I couldn't tell which way it came from but I was also pretty bloody drunk too so I had no idea what I was doing exactly and how I could sort this before it got worse. Well it did get bloody worse as my dad's next door neighbour had seen the commotion and thought she would ring the police.

Obviously I didn't know that at this point so I carried on trying to get Lauren to stand up and collect her shoes from the road. I couldn't do anything as she was just being a complete and utter arsehole, like always. I had decided to run back to my dad's girlfriends' house to get some help with Lauren. It was like five minutes, if that, to run up the road. I got there and explained what was going on to my dad's girlfriend. She said she would come down and help sort it.

We walked down and got outside my dad's house when I saw a police car. My instant thought was 'For God's sake, all I wanted was a quiet one.' A 'quiet one' when Lauren is about is as far from quiet as it is being quiet in a warzone. I remember walking down the path in my dad's neighbours' garden and seeing Lauren and the police officers sat in the front room talking. I thought 'Maybe she's told them the truth about what actually went on and now we can all go to bed and sober up.' How damn wrong was I?

I got to the front door with my dad's girlfriend behind me. I knocked on and then the door swung open and all of a sudden the bloody handcuffs were out and slapped onto my wrists. I instantly said "What the hell are you doin'? I haven't done a damn thing!" They said they were arresting me on 'suspicion of domestic violence'. I blurted out "I am innocent, I wasn't doing anything wrong. I was only helping Lauren get inside because she was drunk as hell." They weren't having none of it.

My dad's girlfriend had asked Lauren what had happened, by this point I was being taken into the back of a police car. Lauren was screaming at the police officers saying "He didn't do anything, he didn't hurt me, it was me, I was drunk and being an idiot." My dad's neighbour had come out also to see what was properly going on. I knew the neighbour from years ago as she is very good friends with my dad, she didn't know I was his son or else it would have been different.

I got put into the back of the police car and Lauren was screaming at the police and my dad's girlfriend was trying to get Lauren out of the road as the police car set off. Lauren had kicked the back of the police car, lost her balance and fell in the road. I remember the police car driving off with me in the back. The handcuffs weighing heavy on my skinny wrists, big chunky metal things they were. I had begun to roll them around my wrists as they were way too tight.

The officer who was sitting next to me had grabbed my hands to stop me from hurting myself. I pleaded that I was innocent and that it was all a big bloody misunderstanding. Nobody believed me of course, that is what hurt me the most. I was just trying to calm Lauren down and get her into the house where it was warm and settled. I had never hit Lauren or done any sort of damage to her physically so I was so damn enraged as to why I was being arrested on 'suspicion of domestic violence'.

The neighbour had rang them and told them a load of bloody shite! So away to the police station I went. Oh and to mention I had never been arrested before so I didn't know what to expect and how long I'd be in for. I was drunk and had the most horrendous of headaches! Probably to do with the tons of alcohol I had drank prior to this whole shitstorm. I arrived at the police station and I was taken into custody where they ask for your details.

You have to take out your piercings, shoelaces and anything that you could harm yourself with whilst you're in police custody. I gave them my details and told them what they had asked for. I had never been in a police station so it was quite an experience, especially with it being New Year's Day. It was still fresh into the New Year, sometime in the morning. I remember walking to my cell, they had escorted me round the other cells and I could smell the freshly cleaned floor. The disinfectant lingered around the maze-like station.

There were bright office-like lights, the long bulb ones the ones you see in colleges and schools. They were dotted around each bit of the ceiling in the station. Everything was painted blue and white, it was very clinical looking too. I had arrived at my cell for the night, it was a big, concrete box-style room. I was greeted with a stainless steel toilet, the 'bed area' was a raised concrete block with a thin, blue plastic mattress that had a grey, cotton blend blanket tossed on top of it. I also remember the grey, pullover police cell jumper.

The cells jumper I wore many times after that night as I had taken many coloured sharpies and created my own pullover jumper with my own 'brand' drawn on. I had written in the middle of the jumper 'STRING TEETH' with some flowers around the writing. String teeth is my art name, I used to use that name for marking my work and basically using it as a brand name. I have always loved the idea of selling my artwork on clothing and using it as a base formation of promoting my work.

That cell jumper is now with somebody else, as I said earlier I have always loved the idea of selling my artwork on clothing. I had sold it for a couple of quid when I was homeless. That is what I did, I sold custom-made clothing to people and made a few quid to buy baccy, food, bud and anything else I could buy at the time. I have made many custom things and now they are all throughout society. One day I hope to have a clothing line, oh the freedom of art. I had also ripped my shirt in half due to a drunken rage whilst in the cell.

That's why I had the cells jumper but I did it due to

the fact I was innocent and had never once broke the law. I have kept my nose clean since though, in my cell I was looking around and I saw there were a window but it was frosted glass so I couldn't see anything outside. Just hear the noises of the free and living. Nothing else to do or to see but hear my own thoughts and look at the off-white walls. Oh God I was so damn pissed off, I remember walking around my cell in a circle. Sort of thinking 'What is going to happen now? When am I getting let out? Can I have a damn cig now?'

Oh honestly not having a cig and not having the freedom to do so is surely a test of one's patience and will power. You truly feel like a caged hen your freedom gone and only your thoughts and feelings to remain. I began feeling drained and ready for bed, I had laid down on the 'mattress'. It was far from a mattress that's for certain, I had closed my eyes and away into the dreamland I entered. Oh don't you love it when it rains heavy and you stare with a hazy mind out onto life.

I had spent my first night in a cell and I awoke to the policeman asking me "What do you want for your breakfast?" I remember ordering an all-day breakfast with a coffee, two sugars and a bit of milk only. The all-day breakfast on the other hand looked as though it was from World War Two and that it had been nuked alongside Japan. It was a brown plastic microwaveable tray with baked beans that were similar to bullets and the mushrooms were soggy and black.

Oh and to make it worse the cheeky bastards said to me "If you don't eat it all up, you can't go home." I didn't eat it all though, I honestly couldn't, I had eaten what I could to soak up the remaining Cîroc and rum in my stomach. I had finished my coffee and all that was missing were a nicely rolled cig with sterling tobacco. I also remember these two old ladies wheeling a book trolley about handing books to those who wanted one. I

45

remember picking up a Biff and Chip book for some unknown reason. I was half-way through it when I was called in for an interview.

I had finally got the chance to smell the 'fresh' air of the clinical disinfectant hallways. I had got into the interview room and there sat the interviewer. He was a sound guy as he knew it was all a misunderstanding. I wanted to get out as quick as I got in so I had just told him the truth. He agreed it was all a big misunderstanding and he let me go without any further comments. I collected my belongings and put back in my sterling silver earring. It took the piss as my fingers were too big for the clip to fasten, I eventually got it in and put on my Harrington jacket, Puma suedes and collected my bits from those clear plastic evidence bags.

I left the station and bombed straight down to the taxi rank by the park at the bottom of Huddersfield town. I jumped in the taxi and on the way back to my dad's girlfriends' I stopped off to collect some cash I had stashed at my dad's. I used the cash to pay for the taxi. I then went to my dad's girlfriends'. I danced up the garden steps and to the front door, I knocked twice and the door opened. Lauren answered and gave me a hug, then I walked through to kitchen. My dad and his girlfriend were sat around the table.

He asked me "What happened?" I told him "It was all a big misunderstanding and that there were no charges." He said "Sound" and handed me a pack of sterling cigs. Back when there were sold in the original packaging, not like today's cig boxes that have horrible images of the effects of smoking. I had got a brew handed to me and enjoyed my cig. I had felt as though I had just been released after a ten-year sentence! I was sat with a cig and a brew, all handed to me as though I had completed a mission. The cigarette had finished and so had my brew.

The days passed, I mentioned earlier about my mother not being happy that I was at my dad's with Lauren. Eventually she'd come round to my dad's and basically explained to him that Lauren is evil, that she is not to be trusted and also that she is a bad influence. My mother also discussed all the other shite that followed Lauren. I knew at this moment that it was all going to end and that it would be time to leave my dad's place. Lauren's parents were also phoned up to come over, they came round to my dad's to speak with us both and try sort the situation out on their side.

My mother had told Lauren's parents about what had happened in Liversedge with the wine bottles, the evil influences Lauren had over me and the period stains on the mattress. Time knocked on and Lauren's parents were wanting to wrap things up and so did my mother and dad. I remember Lauren's mother offering a truce and letting it all go under the bridge. My mother strongly disagreed with a stern voice and said "I am not letting this all go, I do not want to have that girl at mine again."

Me and Lauren went out the back for a cig, we smoked a sterling fag, then hugged and kissed goodbye until the next time. We had finished outside and then we went into the backroom and spoke with our parents. We left my dad's house separately with our parents, I had left my dad's and said thank you to him and my grandad for everything. They said "You could have stopped for longer" but I said "No I wanna leave", then went away with my mother back to Liversedge. Chucking the backpack my grandad had gifted me with into my mother's car boot with the contents of it being a Jack Daniels whiskey bottle, all my clothes from Leeds and my presents from Christmas.

By this time it was like the first week into January 2017. I got a roasting off my mother and I said "Sorry for the shit I have caused but thanks for the presents, love you." Things were moving fast with me and Lauren. Oh very fast indeed. I got back to Liversedge with my mother, my room was all tidied and my clothes all in black bags. My art and all my belongings were intact sat in the last place I left them. I had stopped at my mother's for like a week and then I was asked by Lauren if I wanted to live at her parents' house for a couple of weeks until a more permanent place came along.

I agreed and packed my bag that I used a week or so ago, I remember stood in the living room with my mother. She was tearful, I said "I love you and thank you for everything, I will come and visit you, take care." I hugged her and out the door to Riddlesden I went. Oh this was where the 'wanderer' was born, I have always moved from place to space after leaving my home in Liversedge. I could not find a home like that again once I left that cold January morning. I have lived in Bradford, Huddersfield, Holmfirth, Batley, Leeds, Liversedge and many other places along the way.

I have always been the giver in life. I have always given my all to anyone and anything. I have given my last few quid to a stranger, I have given my last cig to a homeless man. I have fed those before myself as I do not do things for a return. I do them as I know how it is to be without. It just hurts me because I only ask for the same back but I am sorry to say I never do get the equal amount back. Regardless of the person or situation. No matter the person it should always be equal, equality for everyone is what it should be.

For example with girls I have spoken to previously, I have always been the chaser not the chased in that case. I have always been the one to ask after them before they ask after me, never me getting a chase from them. There is this girl that works in my local Sainsbury's. I honestly felt so enthralled by her from the very, very first glance. We had some eye contact and I had this ultimate sense of jelly legs. I basically was anxious as hell, now I know that if you feel 'anxious or nervous of some disposition' then that girl ain't the right one. Apparently you should feel calm, cool and collected.

Anyways, I had been wanting to use the kiosk to buy some cigarettes when she had jumped behind the till to serve me. I thought 'Great, here is my chance to ask her out.' Well I had nervously bought my cigarettes and walked right out the bloody door like a scared little mouse who has just clocked a cat. I thought 'I need to do something fast' so what I did was, I wrote down my number on a piece of paper then had a cigarette to calm my nerves.

I went back in and it was almost like a movie scene. I had walked around the aisles, picked up a Kinder Bueno, a white one of course. I carried it over to the kiosk, now I know she probably thought 'What is this dude doing? He has just been in two seconds ago?' I got to the kiosk and I handed her the Bueno, she asked "Is that all?" I anxiously murmured "No, can I also give you this?" She had accepted my phone number on this ripped up bit of notepad. I said "Thank you and take care", I left Sainsbury's with the biggest bloody grin ever! I felt blessed, I thought 'Go on lad! You did it! You actually had the balls to do it.' I got home and all I could think of was her face and my phone lighting up with a message from her.

A week had passed and I thought 'Maybe I had written my number down wrong or maybe she was anxious too?' My overactive mind had begun its war with my heart, I started thinking all kinds of daft shit. Always was an over-thinker me, anyways a week had gone by and I thought 'This is strange, I have defo wrote it down wrong.' I had come up with the idea to write it down again then go in and hand it to her whilst also making a little convo. I wrote it down a second time, went into Sainsbury's and she was stood in the entrance of the shop.

On her own and easier to talk to, I had asked her "Hi, sorry to bother you but did you get the right number, I was worried it was a wrong number?" She had replied "Oh I am sorry but I haven't had a chance to text you yet." I thought 'Hm okay fair enough, people are busy with their lives.' I had asked her "What is your name?" and "How is your day?" I had thought 'Blessed, I am getting somewhere here.' I handed her the second note, I know I certainly wrote the right number down this time.

She took the note, looked at me then said "My name is Charn." I said "It is nice to meet you Charn, take care, give me a text sometime." I left the store and went back to my flat. I thought to myself 'She has to text me now, she can't not a second time?' I was sat watching *Peaky Blinders* a few hours later when a message came through to my phone. It read 'Hi found your number on the floor, thought you'd be a hottie so I text you.' I instantly thought 'Nah what the hell, found my number on the floor?' She dropped my number on the floor then some other girl had found it and texted me.

I was quite hurt to be honest as I genuinely thought she liked me off the bat. She was friendly towards me, smiled and took my number. She had led me on for a week, believing I had a chance with her. I had actually got my hopes up all week thinking 'Maybe she is just shy or she is working or she is just busy being a young lass.' I never would've thought she would drop it on the floor in her locker room at work for another girl who is her colleague to then pick it up and text me. I was quite pissed off to say it lightly as I didn't want this other girl to text me, I wanted Charn to.

Now Charn walks past my house more or less every Monday and Tuesday on her way to work. She even sometimes glances up at my window as if to say "I fooled you, you ain't gonna have me." To be honest I don't hate her, I still find her beautiful! I am just sick of meeting these girls who just lead me on or they shoot me down good and proper. I have been let down by so many girls it is unreal, I am always the one to be silenced. I admire pure honesty, I am awfully alone if I honest.

Of course every guy wants that one lass to hold at night. Like I said I have always been the giver in relationships, whether friend or girlfriend, I never receive the same treatment I put out. It hurts me to not feel appreciated and adored the way I do with others. I simply do not know what girls want, maybe because I am too nice? Apparently being 'too nice' is bad nowadays, how the hell can being 'too nice' be classed as a bad thing? Society is so twisted and backwards, I simply feel lost within it.

I have stopped looking for love, I am too tired of chasing and wasting time. I want only to fall asleep and wake up beside an angel of my own. Oh well, never mind. I remember when I was quite young as a kid I had been at Wacky Warehouse which was an indoor play area I used to visit growing up. It is now a grill and steakhouse place, I had spent many youthful moments in the play area there. Oh the mixed slush puppies my mother and father bought me as I was leaving the play area after hours of bombing about like a nutter.

I remember one mad incident I had there where I'd fallen off the big blue slide. I had succeeded many times before but this one time I had lost my grip whilst in mid-air, I fell and hit the back of my head on the hard blue plastic slide. I slid down the pissin' slide screaming my head off, I had slipped because there was a rope bridge that went across and above the slide. I used to slide halfway down and jump to reach the rope bridge. I used to swing from it like a spider monkey and all the time over the intercom I would hear "Please stop swinging from the rope bridge and stop messing on the slide."

I remember this chubby kid who tried doing it and he fell like I would do. He banged his head too and oh shit the pain was major! I saw stars and had a crazy concussion, I left with my slush puppy in hand, tears down my cheeks. I felt as though I had had a bowling ball lobbed at my skull. Defo didn't do that again! Oh do you ever feel like you are different to other people, as though you are not from the same place as everyone else? I have always felt as though I am special compared to others, I have never felt like I have fitted in anywhere.

I feel so detached from the everyday life, I don't have the 'normal' outlook on life. All that go to school, then leave and go to college or work. Save for a mortgage and start a family, then spend your days going to work in some job you don't deeply love. Only to make ends meet as you struggle and scrape by to then just rot away. Regretting not doing the things you wanted to do back when you had the chance. It has always scared the shit out of me, I have this fear of failure.

I refuse to be a failure as I do not wanna live and die one, I know in life we fail at certain things and it is up to us to try again until we succeed. I have seen the miserable existences of others and I don't wanna end up like that. I don't wanna sound awful but honestly I have lived many places. These places have shown me the depressingly raw outcomes of life and the bad side of it. Drug use, homelessness, poverty, death, violence, pain, lies, suffering, addictions and more. I have seen what life is like when you give up on yourself, your problems and let them slip away like the wheels of a car on a layer of ice.

I remember being in Batley where I used to live in these flats that were owned by a housing company. Basically a hostel, I lived there when I was nineteen and then I turned twenty there. On my twentieth birthday I had got a rose tattoo. I got it done by the tattooist up the road from the flats. In these flats it was strange because they weren't horrible, like they weren't smelly or were trashed. It wasn't that bad but when you got into people's flats that was a different story.

The flats were basically bedsits, my bed, kitchen and front door were in the same room. Only my bathroom was separate. I lived there for a couple of months, it wasn't too bad but I remember one night me and Lauren had been drinking in Huddersfield. At The Warehouse Bar we had drunk a bit too much so we decided to head back to my bedsit in Batley. We jumped in a taxi, got back to mine and then I remember she had fallen asleep. Bearing in mind before she went to sleep she had been going off on one at me again and causing a domestic like always.

Every place we ever lived in she had always caused issues, major ones with neighbours and people living amongst us, depending on the place. Anyways as she was asleep, I went to look for some bud to buy in the flats so I went knocking on this one flat. I knew this one guy sold bud who lived there and I knew he did heroin and crack too. I knocked on his door and he answered and asked us to come in, I walked in and sat down.

I could see and smell that he was using heroin before I had knocked on the door. He had been using tinfoil, a glass pipe and a lighter to smoke the heroin. It has such a distinct smell, it wasn't a foul smell like shit but it wasn't a sweet smell like cherries. Don't get me wrong I ain't saying it smelled nice, it just smelt weird. I was quite bloody drunk at this point too, I had been drinking gin and tonic's all night and hadn't eaten much to soak it up either.

I bought some bud off of him, then I had rolled myself a joint as I know I couldn't smoke it in my flat as Lauren would've gone crazy and tried killing me or something. She is crazy man! I had smoked my joint, as the night passed on and I was becoming higher and higher from the potent lemon haze. I had got further and further into the intoxicated madness. I had bought two draws of lemon haze so I was rolling, rolling. I remember

53

the neighbour showing me his stomach and he had tiny holes where drugs had eaten away at his insides.

He had said it was from using hard drugs. I think he said heroin or something, it was disgusting to see what drugs actually do to you. It is so messed up! Drugs aren't fun! They mess everything up madly. His friend came down to his flat, I remember this corpse-like man walking in. Grey dreads that were matted, unclean, smelling and rag-looking. He had a hunched back and looked as though he was from the Stone Age. I ain't being mean, but honestly this man was sadly a victim of drug abuse.

I ain't judging him or owt, but he was really messed up, he had said to me "Never try heroin, it messes you up, I have to do it just to feel normal like you." I was proper gobsmacked as I felt so bad for him as I couldn't imagine having to do something like heroin just to feel normal, instead of doing drugs to feel different like a lot of people do. I do not drink or do any other substances now because I have seen what they can do to you and your life. I have had my time with them and now it is time to let it all go!

I try not to regret anything due to the fact of not being able to change it and taking it as a life lesson so next time you know differently. Life lessons are all that regrets are. Don't regret, just let things be. I feel like there are two of me and I am having to get to know both versions of myself. I have to find both versions of myself again, I have not really had a stable image of myself before. I sort of just shapeshift into anything and anyone. I have the ability to become anything or anyone I shift into.

I am many things and many people. I know all kinds of information relating to all kinds of paths. A 'knowledge collector' is what I am, I don't stick to one thing, I collect an array of things. I crave an angel to call my own, I want to hold an angel in my cotton, white sheets. To get lost in the euphoric sensations and pleasures we both hold. Oh I want to wander in your forever-lasting, lovely wilderness wherever you are. I haven't laid beside an angel before, I have only seen them within society but the ones I have craved haven't craved me.

I want to caress and hold her lovely self within my warmth and comfort. Oh I do not know what it is like to be adored, adored like an ancient relic or admired like a Basquiat painting. I am in the shadows of love. Heard but not seen, partially aware of but not truly enough. I remember having to wash my clothes in the bath in Berry Brow, I had never actually washed any sort of clothing in the bath before so it was a bit of a stun to my head as growing up I had always used a washer.

In Berry Brow there were these industrial sized washers and dryers that eighty odd other people used. Now if you have ever been to Berry Brow you will understand that there are some unsavory characters down there. I am not judging but I promise you that you wouldn't want them in your home. I was around criminals, ex and still committing crimes, I was around heroin and crack addicts, I was around the lost and tormented. I didn't want to use the washers as there was blood splattered on the doors and blood all over the floor. It looked like somebody had injected and missed the vein, then squirted blood everywhere. It was disgusting!

I remember one time I was in my flat which was on the top floor, floor sixteen it was. I was writing some of my poems when I heard all this commotion outside. Shouting and screaming is all that heard, I walked onto my balcony and I could see this dude who was bleeding quite badly from his right arm. I had noticed who the guy was and to be honest he was a bit of a mouthy one so I didn't really like him. I then saw this foreign man, he was Middle Eastern or something. This foreign man I saw only a couple of weeks ago in the laundry room as he was asking me for weed.

Anyways he was outside running around the car park away from the dude who was bleeding badly. It turned out the foreign guy had stabbed him in the arm. I had never seen anyone get stabbed or the aftermath of a stabbing but I know that it was quite distressing as there was blood continuously pouring out of his arm. I remember the foreign man darting into his flat from outside and then the armed police turned up with their guns, sirens and riot shields. They pulled out their submachine guns, the gun looked like a G36C, the ones the police use in airports.

They were equipped with riot shields and away they went to arrest the foreign man. I had an idea that he may have killed himself as I remember there was a doctor downstairs who had a stethoscope. I was putting two and two together and thinking 'Maybe the doctor is there to pronounce him dead and take the time of death.' I had not seen the foreign man come out in handcuffs so maybe he did end his life. Maybe he didn't, I don't know.

I have felt weed 'helped' me with my mood and my mental health but honestly it doesn't. I have found that I will get high, then sober up and I will be anxious, broke, craving a spliff and stressed because I haven't got the money for anymore. I have had my fun with smoking weed and drinking but now that I am twenty-two I feel it is time to leave it all behind and start a fresh year without any substances involved. I have smoked weed more than anything in my life, I guess it was my safety net but not so safe after all. I guess I had made myself believe that weed was the medication for me.

I have been on numerous prescription meds and honestly none of them do me any good. Don't get me wrong, if you have to take them or you are taking them and they are helping you then fair enough. For me though, I just think they mask the issue. The issue will always be there, for as long as you are alive it will be there. You have to do some deep, dark, eternal soul search and find what is eating at your core. For example, say if you broke your arm or leg, then you only used morphine for the pain but didn't fix the broken bone itself, what would happen? The broken bone will not heal correctly as you are using morphine to mask the pain but not solve the pain.

It is the same with our minds and hearts. You have to find the source problem, then you have to fight the fight no matter how big or small. You have to truly fix your issue for what it is and not mask it with alcohol, drugs, prescriptions or any sort of unhealthy coping mechanism. I have been there with all three and I can hold my hands up and say 'You will lose'. No person whether rich or poor, happy or sad will ever win against substances. Once you head onto the path of self-destruction and torment you will try and use everything to block out the pain.

It won't eradicate it at all, you will need to take more and more of whatever substance to help ease your pain. I have been there with alcohol, I have drank daily. Liters of the stuff, beer to gin, gin to vodka, from vodka to cider and so on. I have used substances more times than I have had proper relationships. I have done the lines of cocaine, I have took the bombs of MD, I have smoked king ones¹ and cones. I have eaten the speed paste and stayed up for three days, talking to my hallucinations as I stand in my kitchen at 4:00 AM.

I have eaten, sniffed, bombed and smoked my way through my issues but sadly my issues were surrounding me as I walked deeper into myself. They weren't going away with each spliff I smoked or each pill I took or each line I sniffed. They were always there. People seem to think that doing drugs and alcohol is the right way for medicating but I guarantee that those people will either end up three ways; the ground, prison or a psych ward.

I have been in three psych wards before, I was in Ashdale, Halifax in 2018, I spent two weeks there. I was then in Ashdale again in 2019 for about a week and a half, then I was in Dewsbury, Priestley Unit for about two days. I hated Priestley Unit, it was a mixed ward with both female and male patients. The first time I was admitted, was a whole new experience for me as I had never ever been sectioned before. I had only heard about people being in those places.

The first time I was sectioned relates back to when Lauren had cheated on me. I had come home one night back in December 2018, I had been to a mental health appointment with my family. Lauren was there as well, I had no idea that the night before my appointment my uncle had committed suicide. I got home after the appointment with Lauren, back when we lived in Holmfirth. I had no idea that my uncle was dead at this point so I had casually gone about my day. I had been prescribed Diazepam for my emotionally unstable personality disorder.

I had been watching *The Simpsons* all monged out on my medication. Lauren had known about my uncle before me as my mother had asked her not to say anything as they didn't want me to lose my head about my uncle's death. The night came to a close, the next day my mother had picked me up to go visit the rest of my family at my sister's house. We arrived at my sister's and honestly there was this truly dampened feeling in the house, like everyone had lost their hearts.

I remember I sat down on the couch across from my brother, sister and mother. My brother softly spoke the words "Y'know Uncle Martin?" I inquisitively asked "Yeah, what about him?" My brother then nervously said "He killed himself last night." I had not properly processed the news, I sort of sat there thinking 'What the hell do I say? What do I do? This can't be true.' I felt totally lost for words, I remember my family's eyes glaring at me. The way they looked at me with their grief ridden faces, awaiting my response.

I had stared at the carpet, looked around then back up and I said "Bloody hell, why did he do it?" Still to this day we have no clue why he did it but we all do not blame him at all. He himself felt it was the only way out. He must have been in extreme damn pain and that was his final option. I have seen the effects that suicide had on all of us in the family. Grief is such a weirdly awful thing. My family and I for the next few hours comforted one another and sat in completely crushing shock. We were not able to comprehend the whole messed up situation, it was awful.

I wouldn't wish that feeling upon anyone, I slept at my sister's that night so I wasn't at home feeling lonely and depressed. The next day came and I spent it with my family, we were all talking about my uncle's death. It was and still is such an awful stab to the heart. Our hearts have been roughed up and shook about ever since. Later that day I had been taken to a friend's house. I was chilling there for a couple of hours smoking and drinking like any other young adult. I was still in complete awe about the death of my uncle.

The night drew to a close so I returned back to Holmfirth. I remember it was a cold, dark and wet night in December. I had got to the top of my street then felt this tremendously horrible feeling as though something wasn't right. I had this urge to go round the back of my house and not through the front. I crept on down the side of my neighbour's house as that was the only way to my back garden. I passed my neighbour's window, then stood outside my back door.

I had heard Lauren moaning. My blood instantly boiled like a kettle without water. I remember crying, saying to myself "Oh god no, please no! Oh how could she? No damn no! Please do not be true!" I had my few moments of sudden realisation. I then peaked slightly through his window, I could not properly see them both as there was a homemade curtain tied up. I could see that my neighbour had no top on and Lauren was laid down. I could hear piercing moans from Lauren.

They were sleeping together. I felt powerless, weak, disgusted, tormented and fueled with fire and rage. That night I became heartbroken, I remember banging as loud as possible on the window and shouting "What the hell is going on? What the hell are you doing? You damn slut! I am gonna kill you both!" I went completely psycho that night, they both ran to the window and there they were. All bedraggled, sweating and half nude. My neighbour had his trackies on with no top, Lauren had her clothes partially on. I had threatened them both with death.

I cried, screamed and shouted the street down. I was ready to kill them both. She had unlocked the door, then said "I am so sorry, things have been so messed up recently, I didn't know what to do, I am sorry." She peppered me with all of these pathetic excuses. She even had the damn cheek to say "Do you want a cuddle?" Enraged with pain I replied "Get the hell away from me before I rip out your eyes!" The neighbour hadn't said much, he stood like a little bitch with his tail between his legs. He didn't dare talk to me, I had hurled endless abuse at him and her.

They both had said that they did it because they "thought I was already sectioned." I mean how low can two people be? They decided to sleep with each other because they thought I was already sectioned. I was mortified, all the love I gave her, all the memories me and Lauren had were now on the frost covered ground for all the world to see. I lost every piece of love I had for that girl that night. I couldn't believe it, I mean how damn evil? You decide to do it behind my back thinking I was in hospital where I wouldn't have even known. I probably would've never have known once I was out either.

Chapter 4

I do not get how they both can live with themselves. How bloody cruel and soulless. I remember wanting to grab Lauren by her hair and rag her to the ground. I had planned to destroy her face with my fists and my boots. I was gonna kill them both with my screwdriver. No lie! I was ready to murder! Lauren wouldn't come near me and my neighbour had been standing in his crack den of a house. Looking all sheepish and lost for words, I asked her to come with me into my house but she knew as well as I did that if she came into my house that night, she would've left in a body bag.

I had this completely uncontrollable rage inside my blood! A fire inside my soul. I was hurting with this nightmarish pain deep within my heart. I wondered to myself 'How can this girl do this to me? How can she? After everything I have done for her?' I felt betrayed, so bloody, terribly betrayed. I had always done my best for Lauren, always looked after her, cared for her and stood by her. I had always, always put her first before myself. I guess it wasn't love after all, it was just a bad habit I called Lauren.

She never gave me what I gave her, she was never equal to me. I was always putting in ninety-nine percent and she was putting in one percent. She used me, abused me and threw me out with the trash. I felt so Goddamn lonely after that night as how can someone who you have been with for so long and done so much for do such a damn, awfully soul-destroying thing. I have never cheated nor have I wanted to either. I am loyal till I die and even then in death I will stay by your side.

I had proceeded to go into my house. Lauren wandered off into the night with my neighbour somewhere, I locked all my doors and began my suicidal mission. I had started to self-harm by cutting myself with a razor I found in my bathroom. I had cut all up and down my arms, the pain wasn't anything like I had just felt outside that backdoor. I was totally in shock, bearing in mind my uncle had committed suicide a few days before this terrible night. So that was still at the base of my mind.

I had taken a box of Diazepam tablets, a handful of Promethazine pills and downed them all with a bottle of red wine. I had written my suicide note and laid there in the comfort of my white sheets smoking my final spliff as the blood leaked down my arms and into the cotton fibers. I remember falling into a drug induced sleep, then waking up the next day. I was confused as to why I was alive, I was glad I was alive but maybe that was because of the red wine and all those pills in my system, as well as the joint I smoked the night before.

I had actually forgotten what had exactly happened last night as I was far from sober and felt like I was lying on some warm cloud. I had got up out of bed, I looked around and then it all hit me again like a ton of bricks. I had come to the instantly brutal reminder that I had been cheated on the night before. It all sunk in and I began to scream, cry and smash every single thing in my way. I had ran over to my neighbour's house across the street, I was friends with him at the time. He was a few years older than me.

He was sound and probably the only person at that time who was there for me and actually cared. He had always invited me over for a brew or a can, sometimes it was both. He had previously cooked me tea several times, he was such a nice guy and had helped me more than my so called mates. I used to sit for hours just drinking, smoking and eating with my neighbour. He was probably the only decent person on the street at that time, not like my other dickhead neighbour who Lauren had slept with.

The neighbour I had been friends with had told me

before I caught Lauren cheating that she was cheating. I didn't wanna believe him at first, I didn't wanna accept that what he may be saying is true. I was in denial because we always think 'Oh it won't happen to me' or 'Oh no, they would never cheat on me'. It was an awfully horrible pill to swallow, I didn't want to believe any of it. I wanted to just wake up from this nightmare but I was already too wide awake. It was a living nightmare instead.

I truly did admire my neighbour who lived across the street as he always spoke to me for hours about life. We spoke about a huge selection of other subjects including people, society, drugs, our past, mental health and all other kinds of topics. I have always loved talking to people of all ages, places and backgrounds. It is quite refreshing to see and hear new things. My neighbour was telling me about his time in Armley prison and his time in Ashdale which I had never heard of until the next day after that horribly tormenting night, when I was actually on the ward at Ashdale myself.

He had told me about his time in the army and basically bits of his life that were important to him. I had also told him bits from my life too. Getting back to that morning after the cheating incident, I had ran over to my neighbour's. I knew he did speed and was an alcoholic so I knew I could try and get one of the two or both so I could numb this pain I felt. I knocked on his door and asked him for some speed, I took a small teaspoon and swallowed the speed paste. It looked like a clump of marshmallow fluff.

I then asked my neighbour for a sip of his Jägermeister that was stood on top of his microwave. I now felt fueled and ready, I went back over to my house and that is where the destruction of 17 Field Road began. I ran back into my house and I started to destroy everything in my path. I emptied all the cupboards onto the floor. Bowls, plates, mugs and glasses all smashed into pieces, I then punched the cupboards off the wall and they were obliterated. I had thrown my food that was also in the cupboards all over the floor.

I had thrown my microwave around the living room before I threw it against the wall. I threw white paint all over the couch and the walls. I remember throwing my blood stained mattress out in the garden, stained with my blood from the night before. I had then jumped on the wooden slats from my bed and snapped them into pieces. I had thrown all of my personal belongings everywhere and covered them in paint. I broke the shower off the wall and cracked the bathroom tiles. I destroyed all the room doors to the point where I could have walked through the holes I put in them.

I had cut myself some more on my arms and I had wrote 'You have killed me' in my blood on the living room wall. I had used a piece of broken glass and a razor to self-harm which caused tremendous damage. I remember wearing a white t-shirt and it was just covered in blood like I had actually killed Lauren and my neighbour. There were broken glass and egg shells that scattered around the kitchen floor. There was a suitcase that was covered in puncture holes from where I had stabbed it with my blue screwdriver.

I imagined it was Lauren and my neighbour's faces, I had stabbed the couch multiple times. I had gone around punching, kicking and breaking every piece of furniture in sight. I had a coffee table that I threw against a wall and it broke into two. I threw some of my furniture outside and the rest that was left got destroyed further. I had smashed my cups, bowls and plates against the walls, they shattered into pieces. I had finished destroying the whole house from top to bottom. I then sat on the living room floor crying, screaming and bleeding some more.

I feel so bloody bad now as I remember my mother

coming to see me after I had destroyed my house. She knocked on the front door, I had been in my living room at the time laid on the floor. She couldn't get in the front door as there were bowls, cups, plates, food, glass, paint and basically pieces of my life blocking the door. I picked myself up off the floor and exited via the back door. I had walked around the side of the house and there stood my mother. Her face just dropped as though she had seen a ghost, her eyes wide open in instant shock and disbelief.

She had asked me "What has happened Brandon? Why have you got blood all over you? Where is Lauren?" I was in tears and in my hand I was holding my blue screwdriver that was covered in my blood. Now as I look back remembering what my mother saw, she probably thought I had killed them both as I was covered in blood, on my forehead, arms, clothes and hands. She had come round the back and into my house. She was speechless with pain, she couldn't believe her eyes. I had destroyed everything and anything in that house.

She was sadly in a traumatic state, she had asked me "What had gone on? Why have you done this to yourself and your house?" I had explained that I caught Lauren cheating with my neighbour. I told her everything that happened after that saddening event. I remember crying on the living room floor and my mother cradling me, saying "It is alright Brandon" and "Stop crying, it will be fine." I knew in that moment it wasn't fine and it wasn't alright. My mother had tried her absolute best to calm me down and help me stop crying and being angry.

I didn't know what to do anymore, I was broken. I was lost and felt as though everything was over for me. I had never, ever experienced anything so heartbreaking and disastrous before. It was so damn awful. My mother to this day is still shook up by it all and I feel so goddamn badly for that. I never wanted to harm my mother, only Lauren and my neighbour. I am so very deeply sorry to my mother for everything and all that I have put her through. All the tears, pain and anger I have caused her and all the terrible things I have said to her, I am sorry mother, I love you!

I am sorry to my family too for any pain caused to you all. I was just hurting and in a deep depression and darkness. I never meant to hurt any of you intentionally through any of my episodes and my dark moments. I love you all forever and always. I have forgotten a lot of what happened that day in Holmfirth and I am glad I have as it was such a horribly soul-draining day. I remember my mother ringing the police and then an ambulance had also arrived, as it was made aware to the paramedics I had self-harmed quite badly and taken an overdose the night before.

I was in the front garden with my mother, the police and an ambulance crew. I was explaining everything, telling them all the details of the night before and what I'd done the present day. I wasn't arrested as they were on my side and fully understood why I did what I did. Before I had been taken to Huddersfield Royal Infirmary, I saw there was this black bucket that was full of mud, stones and random bits of garden waste. I picked it up and threw it directly through my neighbour's bathroom window which was at the front of his house.

It smashed and all the contents flew out and covered his bathroom floor. I felt a final sigh of relief and shouted "Screw you, you dickhead!" The police officers didn't arrest me either, they didn't charge me with any damages or anything. I was feeling better as I had believed I wouldn't get no justice for the pain I felt. I didn't have my revenge on the night of the cheating incident but now I sort of did. I was escorted into the back of an ambulance to be taken to HRI. I remember being in the ambulance on my own and staring at the floor, thinking 'Oh God, what happens now?'

I was tearful and still fueled on pain, Jägermeister and speed. I was ever so angry, I began picking at the dried blood that covered my wounds. I looked at my arms thinking 'What the hell have I done to myself?' I just felt so pissed off and in despair. I felt an ugly mess. My mother was in her car following the ambulance, the police were also following behind. I felt all kinds of bad, I was in so much pain. Mentally, physically and emotionally. I just felt so done with life.

I got to HRI and instead of me sat in the waiting room I was taken to a different part of the hospital where the paramedics take patients in to be admitted. I was sat in this room with a group of nurses, doctors and my mother. She had sat beside me and made sure I was stable, I had then been booked in by a nurse. I was given a tag with my name, NHS number and date of birth on. I had sat in the admission room waiting to be further examined by the doctors. I had asked the police if I could go for a cig, they allowed me to but only with their escort.

I was escorted outside and began desperately smoking my cig. I was still coming to terms with this whole messed up situation, I finished my fag and went back inside. I was taken to a different room which was isolated from the other patients. I was further examined by the nurses. They had cleaned my wounds and wiped them down. I remember the awfully strong antibacterial fluid they used on my cuts, it was like acid on my skin. I was now waiting for the mental health team to come speak to me.

I awaited on my hospital bed to see what the next step would be. I was laid on the bed with two coppers stood by it. My mother was also present in the room, I was laid there feeling empty, cold and flat. I had had enough, I was just done at this point. I didn't honestly care what happened anymore. Time went by and I remember going outside for another cig an hour or so later. The police had changed shifts by this point and two more coppers were escorting me outside for a cig. I remember walking down the corridors in HRI, there were people staring at me from every corner of the room.

I was covered in cuts and blood stained clothing. No wonder people were staring at me, in that moment I felt ashamed and embarrassed for what I'd done to myself. People kept staring at me with questioning eyes so I screamed out "What the hell are you all staring at?!" I had then kicked a wet floor sign down the corridor and the coppers tightened their grip and pushed my head down to stop me from doing any more damage. Everyone was shook up and didn't say a word. Of course they were gonna look at me and of course I was gonna react like that.

It was just a public reaction to my actions as to why people were staring at me. The coppers said to me "Brandon you have to understand that the reason people are staring at you is because they are shocked at what they are seeing. It isn't to be rude or judgmental." I understand that all now but the way I felt back then I was in no mood for any more shite. Hours passed and it was now time for me to see the mental health nurses.

They invited me to sit down and talk in this clinical looking blue room with these leather chairs. One of them was pink and the other was green. I sat in one of the leather chairs, next to me was my mother and across from me sat two mental health nurses. The police were waiting outside the door, the mental health nurses asked me "What has happened?" They listened to what I had to say then my mother began explaining her part of the story.

The nurses had then said "We are gonna get you into a psychiatric hospital to get you fully assessed and taken care of." I replied "Okay, when am I going?" I wasn't actually that fussed about being sectioned as deep down

I felt it would be necessary and that I needed to have some time to gather my thoughts and feelings. The nurses told me "It will be in the next few hours as we have to wait for a bed to become available." I sat in that small blue room waiting for the mental health nurses to finish assessing me.

I wasn't anxious to be sectioned, I was quite neutral about it all. Time went by and it was like 3:00 AM at this point. I had been in A&E all day and all night, I was still waiting for a bed in Ashdale. I had finally got the green light and the coppers were asked by the nurses if they could take me to Ashdale. My mother had to leave as she hadn't eaten anything since the previous morning, plus she hadn't slept all night. It was now the next morning at around 3:40 AM. She had given me a hug and a kiss then we said "Love you, see you later."

I was then escorted to the back of a police van where I was given a police jacket from one of the coppers as it was freezing. It was off a female copper. She was lovely, beautiful and so kind. I had been given the jacket due to the fact that my white t-shirt was stained with blood and it was wintertime. Oh but nothing was colder than the harsh reality I felt the night before. I put on the jacket and sat in the back of the white metal cage that was inside of the van. The cage was basically a small, white metal box with a plastic screen that you can look through, the seats were metal and it was extremely claustrophobic.

Normally you are taken to the police station but in my case I was sectioned and taken to the psych ward. I remember peering out the windscreen through the plastic screen and watching the night sky. Seeing the stars and the moon glistening down on us all. I then got to Ashdale, exited the back of the van, I was then taken upstairs to Ashdale ward. I had to buzz the intercom to be let in, once I was through the main doors, I walked through to the right then took a left. I was then

71

greeted with two elevators that had a one way entry to them.

When downstairs you can press the button to enter the elevators but once upstairs the only way down was if a staff member opened the elevator for you. I remember getting out the elevator and through the doors to Ashdale ward. That is the male ward, the female ward was called Elmdale and downstairs was for elderly patients, that was called Oakdale. I walked through the doors to the reception, I had to stand in between two sets of electronically manned doors that were on either side of me.

One set of doors went off the ward, the others went into it. Before I went into the ward I had to tell the receptionist my name. They gave me a blue rubber wristband with a plastic black tag on it which unlocked your bedroom door. The coppers had said "Goodbye and take care" to me. I had handed back the lovely police woman her jacket, it smelled like expensive perfume. I felt as though I was wearing my girlfriend's jacket, I felt comforted with it. The coppers left and I was greeted by a staff member at the second doors that went onto the ward itself.

He told me his name but I can't remember it as I was pretty wasted at the time. He was a very friendly and welcoming man. He had shown me to my room and given me some clean clothes. I was handed a green hospital pajama top and some hospital pajama bottoms. They had the words 'Hospital use only' printed a hundred times all over them. I had no clothes as I had destroyed them all in that rage back in Holmfirth. I had thrown my bloodstained clothes in the bin, then I had got into the shower.

The showers in Ashdale were suicide- and flood-proof, basically the showers had a timer so you couldn't flood the place. They had an anti-ligature shower curtain that was magnetically held on so you couldn't hang from it without falling down. The shower had one button only, it was a big stainless steel button. Ones you see in gyms and swimming baths. They were all one temperature and stayed on for like thirty seconds until you had to click it on again.

I remember standing in the shower and looking at the big plughole. It was circular and had huge holes in. I was looking at my cuts and watched the dried blood fall off and entwine with the comforting and warm water. It made a beautiful pinkish colour. It looked like the colour of a sunset in summer, those pink reddish sunsets. I had finished having my shower and put on my hospital pajamas, I heard a knock at the door, it was the gentle, soft-spoken nurse from earlier on. He was holding this small paper cup, the ones you use in McDonald's for ketchup or BBQ sauce.

The paper cup was holding about three small tablets, two were blue and one was white. The nurse had told me they were giving me these tablets to help me sleep and to stabilize my mood. I had swallowed the tablets with a cup of water, I got myself into bed and laid my head on the pillow. It was a single bed and it had a waterproof mattress. The bed sheets were NHS made and they were so friggin' warm to sleep on. The covers must have been made from thermal materials or something because every morning I woke up sweating buckets.

I know that I sweated out the drugs and alcohol as I could smell the toxins on my sheets when I awoke the next day. The beds were so comfy, I felt like I was sleeping on a cotton ball. I awoke and it was around 8:00 AM. I was woken up to the sound of the nurses on the ward chattering and to the sound of the patients letting their chunky wooden doors slam shut, as they wander to the medicine room to collect their morning doses. The nurses were shouting "Breakfast time everyone." I climbed out of bed, then walked outside my room.

I wandered down the corridor to take a look at what

was going on. The food room was a standard looking room with that green hospital lino flooring. It had windows on the back wall that faced onto the car park and into society. It was a tease really, it made you realise you weren't in normality no more. There was a stainless steel food trolley that had milk, cereals, toast, butter and orange juice for all us to dig into. I saw the nurses, doctors and patients who lingered on the ward. I wasn't really up to eating anything as I was still in a horribly depressed mindset.

I had wandered around for a bit taking in the surroundings, I remember seeing pieces of artwork on the walls. They had Van Gogh's daffodil painting on one wall and Gustav Klimt's work on another. I finally got the chance to go for a cig as I had to wait for the other patients to scoff their breakfasts due to security reasons. All patients had to stay on the ward during meal times. I had walked towards the electronically manned doors I spoke about earlier. I asked staff if I could go for a cig, they allowed me to.

Everyone had to hand in their lighters at reception in case there were any arsonists on the ward. Plus it was to stop us from smoking in our rooms but I accidently sneaked one into my room one day. I had turned on my shower, closed the shower curtain, then sparked up my fag. The steam from the shower would mask the smoke which would then exit through the vent in the shower so it wasn't bad at all. I wandered through the electronically manned doors and took a right down the stairs which let outside into the garden.

I got into the garden and there was this green metal shelter that had this circle roof that covered the ground underneath so you wouldn't get wet when it rained. The flooring was part brick paved and part artificial grass. The garden had these big green metal fences, the ones you see in school and colleges. There was no way to escape easily as there were cameras on every corner of the surrounding buildings. I looked up and I could see the windows of the female ward that faced down into the garden.

I didn't see any female patients that day and was intrigued to find out who I was living amongst. I remember one time I was in the garden in Ashdale and there was this Romanian girl who had no teeth and was awfully frail looking. She had said to me "Hey Brandon, you give me money and I will have sex with you. We can have sex once you pay me your money." Her English was broken and didn't make much sense but I certainly knew what she meant when she started mentioning the words sex and money.

She kept trying to goad me into paying her money for sex, basically she was a prostitute on the outside and still her saddening ways had remained inside the walls of Ashdale. I remember she had walked out of the view of cameras, into the corner of the garden. She had then pulled down her leggings and began to urinate against the brick wall. She had piss going down her legs and onto her feet. I was in some proper chaotic place, honestly I ain't judging these poor beings but it truly did send shivers down my spine.

I had walked around the garden, smoked my cig, then I got back inside onto the ward away from the Romanian girl. I went to the tearoom, which was a small shoebox type room with an instant hot water machine on the wall. All that I needed to do was pull a red handle down and there I had my hot water. There were also a fridge for the milk but at times the milk had to be thrown away. There was this old man who wasn't so old living on the ward who looked like an elderly Van Gogh, minus the missing ear.

He used to be a milkman which I found ironic as he would always go into the tearoom and drink out of the milk carton every pissing day. I tried stopping him a few times but honestly he wasn't listening. I knew he had some issues himself as he never spoke a word, he only looked at you with these old blue eyes. Wrinkles all over his face and crow's feet. He was only about sixty-something but he looked about ninety, he wasn't all there. I felt sorry for him because the other patients were quite mean to him for drinking out of the milk cartons.

He would still hold the milk in his hand and drink continuously as he stared at you trying to stop him. He loved his milk did the man. I was in the tearoom and made myself a nice cup of coffee. There wasn't any ceramics allowed so there were only these plastic mugs that came in black and red. They were quite small and burnt your hands when you held the plastic. Not really a thought-out design if you ask me. Anyways I made my brew and wandered down the corridor.

It was one big corridor on the ward, there were these living quarters called pods. Basically pods are hallways where patient's rooms are allocated. There were three other pods including mine, I was in room four and in the second pod. All the bedroom doors were electronically locked so you had to use your wristband to get in. There was a visitor's seating area at the bottom of each pod; a glass room with a couch in that you can use when family or friends come and see you.

I remember being in Ashdale for around two weeks that first time as it was December 2018. I spent Christmas and New Year's in a psych ward. I had met some interesting characters within the wards. I met one guy who was an ex-construction worker and he had two great big scars going across his neck. I had asked him "What happened to you mate? If you don't mind me asking." He replied "I heard voices telling me to hurt others and to cut my own throat." He had cut his own throat due to hearing voices, in his eyes you could see that he was tormented.

He was troubled deeply. He was so friendly and calm

towards me, he never hurt me or said anything horrible. Probably because he was so doped up on meds though, it was sad to see the many souls wandering the hallways. Saliva dripping from their mouths, groans and grunts echoing the halls. I remember this woman who was outside in the garden one day. She sat next to me and had such a sweet voice. She was around fifty-odd and I don't know what her mental illness was but she kept saying to me "I can see faces on my legs, I can see people in front of me." There was nobody there but me and her.

Her eyes looked like portals to the other world, like demons had a grasp on her mind. She was terribly troubled. I remember one day I was outside in the car park at the front of the hospital. That same woman had been out with a member of her family. She had squatted in a corner by the bins and began urinating in full view of society. I never had an issue with people in those places, we were all in there together and through one big reason - our minds. It had opened my eyes to life and to mental illnesses.

I had never seen such tormented beings before. I remember meeting this man in there who had a missing index finger, long greasy matted grey hair and a walking stick. I had asked him "Why do you have a missing finger mate?" He replied to me "I cut it off when I was high on crack, I can't remember doing it as such but I know I got the sharpest knife out of the kitchen drawer, then chopped it right off." I looked at him in a complete state of shock and horror!

That same man had further told me "When I was younger my dad used to sexually abuse me, one day he tried to rape me in front of the fireplace, I could see that there was a small axe used for chopping up wood as we had an old fireplace that ran on wood, I had luckily managed to grab the axe and before my dad could pull down my trousers I had swung around with the axe in hand and hit him in his arm. I could see that I had chopped off his right arm, he then fell to the floor screaming his head off."

I had just sat there with this look of pure terror and sympathy on my face, I have never heard such a disturbing story before. I couldn't imagine the pain this poor man's felt, I don't think I want to either. Ashdale seriously opened my eyes to the minds and lives around me. I remember this other guy who was very 'different', he used to mutter words to himself. He would laugh at the walls and at nothing... literally nothing was there to laugh at.

I remember he had told me "Freddy Krueger is living next door." I had started to laugh at this remark but then I twigged on. The women's ward was called Elmdale and there is that film from the eighties called *A Nightmare On Elm Street*. I mean it was a funny thought-out joke to say, he was doped up and having hallucinations. He then said to me "I just wanna go back to Hebden Bridge in my tent so I can smoke my crack pipe and take my e's." I mean each to their own and all that but bloody hell, in a tent taking e's, smoking crack?

No bloody wonder he was in Ashdale. He had these dark, laughter-filled eyes, very mischievous looking. Sort of like he was possessed by a demon who was a comedian. He looked evil within his eyes and smile but he wasn't. He was just tormented... like a lot of them are. I remember eating the food at Ashdale. It was like eating school meals, there was mash, peas and fish fingers with chocolate cake and custard for afters. Then there was chicken, mixed veg and gravy, then for afters there were rice pudding and an orange juice carton to wash it all down.

The meals were really filling, you could eat and eat until you couldn't no more. I remember eating seconds and thirds at times because the medication I was taking was stimulating my appetite. I put on a lot of weight in Ashdale, I was eating breakfast, dinner and tea every day. Once I came out into the unstable life I went in with, it all changed and I stopped eating properly and was smoking more and more weed. I guess looking back now weed did affect me quite badly. I was just in denial.

I was drinking and doing other substances on occasion too. I didn't lead the healthiest of lifestyles. I was around losers, deadbeats and addicts, they had no goals or dreams. They just wanted to 'chill out man' and self-medicate. Honestly I had no true friends throughout those times, I guess they were all wrapped up in their own minds. I had met many people in Ashdale who had been using drugs and alcohol to self-medicate. Many of them told me "Whatever you do, don't try heroin."

I saw their bodies and their minds everyday more or less. There were people covered in scars, bruises, cuts, burns and other self-harming wounds. I saw their minds stretched out in front of me. Hallucinations, screaming, anger, frustration, pain and sadness. People wiping their nose contents onto furniture, saliva dripping from their mouths as they talk to doors and walls. I honestly have seen it all.

I remember this one woman who was heavily warped by her ill mind. She was outside in the garden and I remember her saying a load of jumbled drugged up sentences. A few of those were "I cut off his penis, he won't take her away." "I will find a way." "They are following me everywhere." "Don't dare come near me, I will stab you." The poor woman was wandering around with bare feet and looked like she hadn't slept in over ten years. She looked severely worn out and messed up. She looked like she had been to the plains of hell and back.

She was smoking cigarette, after cigarette, after cigarette. She was definitely not gonna live normally, I felt so bad because I saw a lot of women in there who were depressingly losing to their battles of the mind. I remember one woman who was about sixty and she was telling me "I have been struggling for over fifty years and I still haven't found the right medication yet, it has taken me ten years to just get here." Her eyes were really dark and had sleepless bags that probably were older than me. She looked like she had given up on life if I am honest. She didn't look happy at all, it was like happiness was a myth to her.

I remember this one nurse who was on the ward when I was there my second time. She was only twenty years old, I was twenty-one at the time. She was a year younger than me and she was dealing with mental health patients at that age. I mean she truly didn't know what to say or do when I was having a crisis in there. I ain't having a go but she clearly wasn't experienced enough to be on a psych ward. She even said "I do not know what to say to you Brandon" and "I am stuck on what to do for you." I know she was straight out of university.

She hadn't lived much due to being at uni. That is why I still now to this day believe that a percentage of people at uni have no life skills at all. The ones who have left school, then gone to college, then uni. They have no bloody brains at all. I have lived through so much and it wasn't from being safe and sound at college or uni. It was from being out there in the wastelands of life and truly living in the shit. I have experienced a lot, even people older than me have had no clue about the things I've spoken about.

They have looked at me as though I am an alien. I guess that is why now I don't have friends or anything because I am such a mature-minded person compared to a lot. They have nothing in common with me as I have had to grow up faster than the majority. I feel sorry for those who haven't lived through any sort of shit or horrible ways of living. I mean imagine not knowing anything about the way the world is, how boring life would be. I know I say this now but I know in those times of despair I was wishing to not be experiencing it at all.

I am grateful for the knowledge and the strength I have collected throughout my young years. I have met people in my life who can't use a washing machine or turn on an oven. I mean how bloody ridiculous? I have been using a washer and cooker since I was about seven years old. How can one go through life and not know these basic living requirements? I have always, always felt different to the rest, I just never relate to others. I once read somewhere that if you feel like you don't fit in this world it is because you are here to create a new one.

I can totally agree with that because everyone else is just so happy plodding along and just doing the same shit on a different day, forget that. I wanna be someone and make myself known in the world. I don't wanna live and die in my hometown, I don't wanna waste away in some job that doesn't pay me well. Wake up every morning wishing to be someone and something else. I wasn't put here to just roll over and die some unknown being. I wanna be on television, Instagram, the internet and YouTube.

I wanna be someone who is remembered for their hard work and suffering. Someone who inspired millions, I wanna be someone who leaves this world a better place. I wanna be someone who is admired, adored and appreciated by many. I have not gone through all that shite for nothing. I know some people just accept it and live out their days in depression and regret but nah that isn't for me man. I wanna tell my story to the world and leave my mark on this earth for all eternity.

I remember when I lived in this hostel in Huddersfield. There were all kinds of evil people living amongst me, I remember this one guy who was in the hostel because he was chased out of his hometown. He had brutally killed a dog, he was apparently doing drugs at the time it occurred but I don't know exactly what happened. I know that he had stabbed the dog and hit it with a hammer until it was dead. I mean how bloody sick can someone be? I heard he'd gone to an appointment whilst leaving the dog to die from its injuries.

He then came back home, tried burying it and then got caught. I don't know how he got caught but he did. He was named and shamed then was chased out of his hometown, I have no sympathy for him. That same guy had been living upstairs from me and on occasions he would ask me for cigarettes. At one point he came into my room as I was in the kitchen next door. It was like being amongst a set of devils. I had left my room to make a brew in the communal kitchen. After I made it, I took the mug and then I opened my room door.

I caught the dog killer looking underneath my pillows and my bed. He jumped so damn high as I caught him searching for my tobacco. I had said to him "What the hell are you doing?" I pulled my tobacco out of my pocket and he turned tomato red in his face. He was so embarrassed, he then left my room in shame. I had to store my food within a blue plastic box inside my wardrobe. People kept stealing my food, coffee and basically anything I put in the communal cupboards. We then had to have padlocks on our kitchen cupboards as people were thieving.

I had begun storing my stuff in my wardrobe. I had to buy powdered milk as it kept going off or being drank. I remember the dog killer stealing my chocolate cake off the dresser in my room. I left my door unlocked, plus I was stoned and didn't notice my chocolate cake was missing. I didn't think my bloody cake would be stolen! The bastard had left my room with my cake stuffed down his pants. I mean hell, just ask me for a piece, not take the whole damn cake. I had to be more careful from then on as I didn't trust anyone around me.

Chapter 5

I had to sleep with a knife under my pillow and carry it daily just in case I was attacked whilst living there. The reason being was because there was this terribly evil guy living on the top floor of the hostel. He was a meathead with a psycho mindset. He had noticed me using the communal dryers at the bottom of the stairwell one day and started to chat to me. I didn't think anything of it as you don't expect to be around evil minded people. He was a horrible, disgusting and sick person.

He had asked me to chill with him and because I am too damn nice I said "Yeah man no worries." We were chilling in his room and he started telling me about himself. He told me he had been in prison for twelve years because of kidnapping and severely torturing someone, he was not a nice man at all. He was telling me stories of when him and his mates did all kinds of shit. I remember he was telling me that him and his friend had seen this random guy walking in the street at night. They'd robbed him of his phone and the guy tried to stop them but they had turned around and knocked him out.

The guy had hit his head and was in hospital. The guy's girlfriend had rung the stolen phone and because it was now in the hands of the meathead psycho he answered it. The girl screamed down the phone "My boyfriend is in hospital now and he is severely hurt. How can you be so evil? Do you know what you have done?" The meathead was just laughing as he told me this story, he was so evil-minded. Another time I remember him telling me "If you wanna mess someone up for life, throw acid in their face as they will have to wake up every day and see themselves like that in the mirror."

I mean how damn disturbed can one person truly be? I felt sick talking to him. He didn't care for anyone or anything, he was so messed up beyond repair. I remember one day he had asked me to come to his room and so I did. I was easily led at one point in my life. He had laid out three little bags on his table, little clear bags you get when you buy weed or coke. He had told me it was coke and MD in these bags, I checked them out. I had seen that it was not coke or MD. It was some other crystal type substance.

The 'coke' looked too white and had little clumps in the bag, I didn't want them, nor did I take them. He said "Take them, you want these don't you? I am helping you out. They are for you. You owe me money for these now though." I replied "Nah I'm alright mate, I don't want them, I don't need them thanks." He persistently attempted to push them onto me. He kept saying "No you are taking them and you owe me now!" Obviously at this point I was pretty stuck on what to do as he had locked his door and was ten times bigger than me in width and height.

I didn't know what to do, I told him repeatedly "Nah I am okay mate, I don't wanna take them." He was having none of it, he kept threatening me and tried to push the 'drugs' onto me. I knew they weren't drugs, he was just trying to extort money from me whilst using his size to intimidate me. I felt trapped, he kept threatening me, trying to get inside my head to manipulate me so I would take the 'drugs'. He said "If you don't use them, you still owe me money." What the hell was I to do?

I ended up taking the bags down to my room out of absolute fear. I got into my room then opened up the bags and poured out the contents onto my glass table. I looked at them closely and under my desk lamp. The 'MD' was an industrial style chemical and the 'coke' was glue that had been dried and bashed up to look like coke. I knew very well that it wasn't coke and MD. I had flushed them instantly down the toilet but oh that wasn't the end of it. I went to his room and told him "I have just looked at the bags and that is not coke or MD."

He had looked at me and said "You owe me money for those now, I don't care." I was bloody trapped in a web of fear, isolation and torment. I told him multiple times I can't pay you and that I didn't take them and that I never wanted them. I was in fear as this guy was a bloody psycho man! He'd been in prison and done messed-up shit. I didn't know what to say or do in that moment and he just said "I want my money for them when you get your universal credit." I wasn't gonna bloody give him money for chemicals and industrial-style glue.

What the hell was I to do? I left his room after like half an hour and went back to mine with this horrible feeling held over me. I honestly didn't know what I was gonna do. There was staff working every day in the hostel but even they were petrified of him. You couldn't do anything as who was gonna stop him? I remember him asking me one time to come and help me with something. This was before the drug pushing incident. He had asked me to help him with something so I agreed being the nice person that I am.

I mean looking back now, I should have never have got involved with him. Hey ho, I was damn stupid and weak back then. He asked me to come for a walk outside with him and in that moment I thought 'There is defo something strange going on here.' We walked down this public footpath to this big wasteland type area. There was this motorbike there and it was not a bad motorbike at all, it was fairly new and was in good condition. He had asked me to hold his phone torch over the ignition of the bike. He had got a piece of metal and tried to break into the lock of the bike.

I nervously held the phone light over the ignition as he attempted to rob the bike. I knew it was so damn wrong doing it, I shouldn't have agreed to but again I was in fear and he got into my head. He tried and tried to steal the bike but failed. Thank God! I didn't wanna be wrapped up in that shit. I wasn't a thief before that and I am not one now. He had stopped trying to steal the bike and we wandered back up to the hostel. He had gone to his room and I went to mine. In that hostel I was so tormented and pushed about.

I felt suicidal at points as I just had enough with the toxic environment I was in. The meathead I was talking about earlier on had come down to my room this one time and started to take my belongings. He had stolen my Doc Martens, grooming kit, electric shaver, dressing gown, coats and jackets. He took a picture frame that had my art in it. He took my mobile phone and a tablet I was using to watch films on. He took mostly everything in my room, carrying it all in my duffle bag to his room.

I remember him saying "I best put it all in this duffle bag because I don't want the cameras to see what I have taken." He was such an awful person! I honestly couldn't stop him, he was just a big disgusting bully. After he left my room I had smashed it up out of frustration and torment. I felt weak and couldn't tell anyone because I knew I would get a backlash from it and that nobody was gonna do anything anyway. He had literally stripped my bloody room bare. I had started to cry in frustration, I didn't know what to do anymore.

I remember not even telling family or my mother as I didn't wanna get them involved and cause them more shit. I honestly couldn't go to anyone. I had to just accept it and move on. Time went by, I remember this one time I was in my room and Lauren had text me 'I am coming over'. I was quite confused as we hadn't really been talking much as we were on a break. When she arrived, she was absolutely pissed out of her head. I didn't actually think she was gonna come all the way from Leeds.

I mean she said she needed to stay somewhere and obviously thought it would be a good idea to turn up at my hostel. This was a hostel and I wasn't even allowed people in past a certain time. Never mind staying over, I was stood in my room and then my buzzer rang, it was Lauren. I remember telling Lauren to be quiet and to calm down as when she is pissed she would become violent and aggressive. There were two people who were in the communal kitchen next door, one of them had knocked on my door.

I knew the person at my door and I also knew the other person in the kitchen. The other person in the kitchen wanted to talk with me. I told Lauren "Two mins, I will be back." I went into the kitchen. The guy who asked to talk with me had started going off on one and began being all angry towards me. I don't know why he was like that towards me but I know a week or so ago I had told him in a friendly manner, it wasn't done with evil intent, that his girlfriend had a look of Lauren.

I wasn't being a dickhead or anything, I didn't mean it in a bad way. I said it because she honestly did have a look of Lauren, he had taken offence to that and started going crazy at me in the kitchen. I had been drinking earlier on and was a little drunk. The guy who was going crazy at me slapped me once or twice then hit me in my groin. I was proper confused, I didn't know what to do. He was much bigger than me and older. I had said "Sorry for offending you" and "I didn't mean anything by what I said."

I literally did not do anything wrong, he was just pissed off because he was a negative guy in general. I was just too nice and had to accept the shit situation. I never went out and caused shit on purpose, it was always to do with someone else. I am not a troublemaker, I hate drama. Anyways, I left the kitchen after that heated moment and I went back into my room to continue talking with Lauren. All of a sudden there was another knock at the door.

It was someone else who was living in the hostel, they said "Brandon let us in mate, I am not gonna hit you or anything, I just wanna talk with you." As I had just been slapped about and punched in the groin there was no way I was gonna let this person in. I had asked Lauren to shut up and help me barricade the door. I had moved an armchair behind the door handle, I had then pushed my bed in front of the armchair so it was properly barricaded. I was proper bloody anxious and felt like I was gonna be attacked.

I don't quite know how it all came about but I know that the dog killer was going around the hostel and telling people I had my girlfriend in. He was such a shit-stirring bastard, he thrived off of drama, like a negative leech. Sucking on the negativity of others. He was a complete twat. I hated it there in that hostel, I honestly hated it! Anyways we had barricaded the door but then more people had come to my room. They began banging on the door and causing shit.

I remember them kicking, punching and hitting it with things. It was like an angry mob outside my room, all for what though? I didn't do anything but have my girlfriend in. I honestly think it was because they were all jealous, bored and wanted to cause trouble for me. I remember Lauren being a bit shook up as the two of us didn't know what to do or where to go. The people outside my door weren't going away anytime soon. I had come up with the idea to leave through the window in my room.

It went onto the street above as my room was in the basement of the hostel. Me and Lauren slipped through the window, then climbed up the side of this concrete wall that went up and over to the road above. I gave Lauren a hand up the wall. The two of us pelted it down the street and away from the hostel, Lauren wanted to buy alcohol... as always. Anyways we went to the shop down the road and picked up some apple-flavoured Smirnoff vodka. We stumbled back to my hostel room and we climbed down the concrete wall.

As I was climbing down I had dropped the vodka bottle and into a million pieces it shattered. The vodka was gone, the two of us groaned in frustration and carried on climbing through my window. We got into my room and sat ourselves down on the bed. Lauren asked "What shall we do now?" I had said to her "I have these pills that help me go to sleep", basically sleepers. Anyways we had begun eating the sleepers like they were cough sweets, because they were so strong the two of us began feeling weird and extremely monged out.

I don't even remember falling asleep but the next morning came, I remember waking up and my hands were shaking from withdrawal symptoms. Me and Lauren had left the hostel and walked to McDonald's in Huddersfield town centre. We got to McDonald's and ordered a coffee each. I remember us sat there feeling like addicts, shaking by the hands and slurring our speech. I felt like I was still asleep and dreaming, everything felt so strange. I know it was damn stupid to take all those sleepers but honestly in my head at that moment in time I was so depressed and done with life.

Mine and Lauren's relationship wasn't great and neither was the relationship I had with my mother and family. I was a mess at that point, I had been acting like an idiot. I was just being self-destructive, destroying my life and all the relationships within it. I feel so bad as I have put my family and my mother through hell and then some. I have acted so out of order and so terribly wrong. I never meant to hurt anyone intentionally, I was in a truly depressed and self-destructive mindset.

I didn't care for myself, never mind other people. I had seriously had enough with life as it was just one thing after another. I couldn't deal with certain things happening and the way my life was. I felt like I was in the abyss and I couldn't ever get out of it. I remember one time I had been laying on the floor in my hostel room, rolling about, crying and feeling absolutely terrible. I felt so sad, like suicidal-level sad. I wanted the ground to swallow me up so I didn't have to deal with life no more.

I just wanted to be a kid again, innocent, free and not lost. Oh I am truly better now though... time went by and I remember I was in the hostel one day and the meathead guy who had told me weeks ago "You owe me money for the coke and MD" had come back from being out somewhere. He asked me to come to his room and talk, I went to his room and he was asking me "Where is my money? When can you sort the money out?" I told him "I haven't got anything" and that "I don't know when I can sort it."

I honestly wasn't going to give someone money for something I didn't take, use or have. I flushed the bloody chemicals and glue down the toilet. I had told him this but he still pestered me to get him his money. He was basically a big bully and thought he could push things onto people and manipulate them. He used his prison mindset on people and used his muscles to intimidate weaker people. He was a horrible, horrible man. I had left his room after about half an hour of constant lies which I told him so he would back the hell off.

I left his room and went back down to mine and sparked a cigarette. I sat in my armchair, crying with mental pain. I didn't know what to do, I literally felt like I was in prison with these devils and that nobody could save me. It was extremely awful to have lived there. I wouldn't ever wish what I felt and went through in that place on anyone. I remember one night the meathead had been drinking vodka upstairs with two other people from the hostel. They invited me up as this was in the first few weeks of me living there.

I thought 'Great, I have made some new friends here.' Oh how bloody wrong was I. I got upstairs into the room where they were, I remember talking to the three people who were in that room. One being the meathead, he had asked if I wanted a drink of his vodka and of course being depressed and lonely I said "Yeah please mate, I'd love a glass." I was given a glass and down the hatch it went. The drinks had flowed and I had smoked a little joint with one of the other people in the room.

I drunkenly slurred out "I used to do boxing as a kid." That is when I realized I should not have said a word as the meathead replied "Oh really? I bet you can take a punch from me then?" I had said "Nah nah, you're alright man, I don't wanna take a punch from you." He was a meathead and a bloody psycho after all. He wouldn't leave it be. I ended up putting my hands above my head and tensing as hard as I could so that his punch wouldn't hurt me as much. I remember him counting down and every time I said "Woah woah, not yet", he would say "Come on man stop being a bitch."

I didn't want to be punched in the ribs by a meathead who was under the influence of drink and God knows what else. I remember he had punched me quite hard as I had fallen onto the bed behind me and was badly winded. One of the other people in the room said "I heard something crack when he hit you." I feel so stupid because of all of that, I just felt like I was literally a punching bag for others. I was manipulated, deceived, fooled and treat like an idiot for the duration of my time in that hellhole of a hostel.

I had no friends in there at all, just disgusting examples of 'human beings'. There was no human in that place, just a bunch of demons. I remember this one night a few of us from the hostel who were sort of alright with each other went to Halifax for New Year's Eve. At this point it was 2017, going on 2018. I had taken some money with me to buy my drinks and for the taxi home later on.

We had gone into a few pubs, I was drinking gin and tonic and having a decent time out.

The night got on and I remember buying some coke off a couple of guys outside this pub. It was pretty strong stuff and it did the trick but oh wow it wasn't great towards the end of the night. I remember being kicked out of the pub for doing coke in the toilets, yes I know it was out of order and I should not have done it. Again I was on a self-destructive path and wanted to block out my shit instead of dealing with it head on. I got kicked out the pub, then the people I was with had all left me and went somewhere else.

I felt a bit anxious and worried as I didn't have any money to get home, my fault I know. I was off my face and was being a total arsehole. I had managed to get to another pub when I saw the people I was with earlier on through the window. I tried to get in but the bouncers wouldn't let me in and told me to go away. I was purely screwed at this point, I didn't know where to go or what to do. I remember walking down the back of the pub that the people from my hostel were in. I was smoking a cigarette as I anxiously waited for them to come out.

They never did and they didn't give a damn about me. I felt proper alone at this point. It was the countdown to 2018, I could hear everyone shouting "10, 9, 8, 7... HAPPY NEW YEAR!", followed by cheers and screams of joy. I had just missed the countdown and was still down the back of this pub. I saw this lass who was wearing a white blazer, white jeans and blonde hair. I got chatting to her, smoking a cig as we were talking. She said to me "Do you want a blowjob?" I laughed nervously then said "Are you serious? Do you actually mean that?" She replied "Yeah come on, let's go down here."

I anxiously followed this girl as never in my life has someone ever offered me a blowjob randomly in the streets. I mean anything could have happened, it was a proper strange experience. We had got down this alley way and she did her thing, she had shown me videos on her phone of her sleeping with men. I was so very confused, I have never ever been in such a weird moment like that before. Anyways, I remember these people who worked at this club. They came out the fire exit from the back of the kitchen for a cig break.

The kitchen had lead into the alleyway where I was, with that girl. They had come out and said "We know what you are doing, get away from here." Scared for my life, I rapidly pulled up my pants as I pelted down the alleyways back onto the streets. The girl had buggered off somewhere else. At this point I was starting to worry as I didn't know how I was gonna get home and who I was gonna call to help me out. My phone was gonna die and I was proper shitting it thinking 'I am gonna be lost in Halifax till the morning.'

I remember having to ring my mother to see if she could lend me a taxi fare home. I explained the situation, that I was stranded in Halifax. She had wonderfully agreed and sent me fifteen pounds to get home. I jumped in a taxi to Huddersfield, then back to my hostel room. I got in and Lauren had rang me asking if she could come over. I agreed even though me and Lauren weren't actually together at this point. We were on a 'break'. I wanted the company, I suppose I wanted to get back with her at some point when I was right and when we were both sorted in our own lives.

She came over and I had explained all what had gone on in Halifax. I remember lying in bed with her and falling asleep till the next morning. I was safe and sound at last. Time went by and I remember having to flee the hostel one night as the meathead psycho didn't get his money from me. I wasn't gonna pay the guy any money for dried up glue that had been bashed into powder and I wasn't gonna give him any money for damn industrial chemicals. I remember one night packing all my belongings and clothes, then fleeing the hostel to start a fresh.

I had gone to a friend's house until the next day when I went to the council and sorted another hostel place out. I hate night outs and all that shite now, it is such a waste of money and health. I literally prefer to stay in and relax rather than go out and be a drugged up idiot who is drunk and disorderly. I have been on many nights out and honestly I can now say that I truly do not care for them. I do not care for drink or drugs no more. It is all a pure waste of everything. My advice to anyone is don't start drinking and definitely don't do drugs.

It is honestly the most stupidest of things to do. It is a waste of your life and your money. It doesn't help your mind, body or wallet. It doesn't help anyone in the long run. I have had my time and experiences with them both. Now I look back and think 'I am so bloody glad I don't drink and do drugs no more seeing how I used to be.' I have made many mistakes and done many stupid things from being intoxicated through drugs and alcohol. Don't start it, honestly! I don't regret things but I used to do.

There is no point in me regretting anything as I can't change it, it has happened, been and done. The past is the past, long dead and buried. As long as you don't carry your past into your present then you will be fine. Each time that you go back and start it all up, you massively increase the negatives effects it does to your mind and body. You lose sleep, money, friends, family and everything good that is in your life. It will take it all away, then one day you will wake up and have nothing and nobody around you.

Honestly I have turned my shit around but before I did, I selfishly hurt my mother and family many damn times. I have lied and caused so much shit through me being an arsehole, doing drugs and drinking. You must get a hold of it or else you will literally lose your mind and everything in your life. You just have to go to Pigeon Park in Huddersfield town centre and there you will see the effects of drink and drugs. You will see the depressing lives of those lost to their addictions.

I have not been crazily addicted to drugs or alcohol but I have had my fair share of using them too much and destroying my life through it all. I have turned it all around now though, I have had enough of the hangovers, the debts and the pain it causes to the loved ones around me. I have never been addicted to a certain drug but I have been addicted to the false safety net it holds under you though. Doing drugs and alcohol gives us all a false sense of comfort, it will never, ever help your issues.

It is a terrible thing to use as a way of coping. Drugs and alcohol only mask the issue, never solve it! I am speaking from experience as I have tried to mask my issues many times and it has never worked. You end up doing more and more and more, until one day you either overdose or you end up in prison through stealing to pay for your habit. You will lose everyone and everything if you use drugs and alcohol to the point of addiction. Honestly you have to get the help and fight it day in and day out.

You will have sleepless nights, you will have withdrawal symptoms and you will have those days of despair and pain. You have to fight it before it beats you into the ground, literally! I have lived an eventful life that's for sure. I have had to wear three jumpers and two pairs of trousers, which were then tucked into two pairs of socks as I lay in my flat with no heating or hot water. With nothing but condensation coming off of my hot breath. I have been sat there eating cold custard out of a tin can because I haven't had food to eat.

I have hand washed my clothes in the bath multiple times and had to dry them on a homemade washing line that I strung up over the bath. I have gone days without hot water, heating and food. I have begged for cigarettes off strangers and stole sandwiches and drinks to survive on a daily basis. I have been sat on the isolated train station steps drinking bottles of red wine to numb the cold night and the pain I had inside me. I have gone to bed wearing wooly hats and jackets so I don't freeze in the night.

I have had to break down cigarette butts to make a cigarette in those desperate times. I have gone days without showering or brushing my teeth. I have lost weight on a daily basis due to me being malnourished and broke. I had to put water in my porridge as I had no milk. I had to put water in my milk just so I can have that last brew or that final bowl of cereal. I had mice living in my hostel room that were chewing up my clothes and eating my food bank supplies.

I had to sell my clothes to get food and tobacco in the most horrendous of times. I had sleepless nights holding knives in my hand, on edge thinking I would be attacked in my sleep. I had my food robbed from other hostel goers. I had my shoes robbed and my clothes taken out of the washing machine piss-wet through. I had knives pulled out on me and threatened with violence. I have woken up alone on the concrete, under the sky.

I have cut myself with razors and knifes and I have burned myself with cigarette butts in an attempt to numb this mental pain. I have drank myself into oblivion and woke up in hospitals. I have woken up with my phone being robbed and my money taken. I have sat on the wards of psych units and cried in pain and isolation. I have been hanging there feeling the life drain from my body as the bedsheet noose is tied around my neck. I have seen my blood countless times on mattresses and bedsheets.

I have woke up in pools of my own vomit from overdosing in my sleep. I have put holes into walls and doors, God so many bloody times. I have broken TV after TV and phone after phone. I have smashed tables and chairs up and I have stabbed holes in my clothes and belongings. I have walked miles and miles, blistered and battered my feet in a desperate attempt to find myself some happiness away from the pain. I have taken overdose after overdose wishing to be someplace else.

I have seen the needles of heroin enter the veins of those around me and I have seen the crack smoke dance throughout the hallways of places I were living in. I have seen people overdosing and rolling on the floor, screaming for help and vomiting on themselves. I have seen people get battered to the point of unconsciousness by a gang of thugs, blood pouring from their noses and mouths. I have had to sprint away from being stabbed and robbed by loads more people than I.

I have seen my ex-girlfriend overdosing in front of me, eyes rolling back whilst in an uncontrollable seizure. I have hurt my mother and my family through my own suffering. I have lied, deceived and been selfish to others. I have woke up wishing to be dead and I have gone to sleep hoping I die. I have been cheated on, attacked, beaten, hurt and screwed over so many damn times. I have contemplated suicide more times than I have had hot dinners. I have seen myself jump off buildings and I have seen myself hanging.

I have seen myself dead on the floor but all that I saw was what could've happened to me. The sick and twisted visions that haunted me as I slept, waking up sweating and panting in fear and illness. I have hated myself and I have loved myself. I have been my own best friend and my own worst enemy. I have sat in my flat with nothing but a bed. I have sat there with suicidal thoughts racing through my head. I have been abused and beaten by someone who claims they love me.

I have wanted to slit my wrists and end myself. I have wanted to take all those pills and not wake up. I have tossed and turned in my bed due to the hellish nightmares I have envisioned. I have burnt many bridges and ruined many things. I have been sat in complete darkness with nothing but a million thoughts charging through my mind. I have gone hungry and without countless times. I have spent all the money I had on drugs and alcohol just to stop the damn torture inside.

I have wandered the streets at night with nobody to phone and nobody to hold. I have cried, screamed, smashed, hurt and been destructive in so many damn depressingly awful ways. I have taken countless medications and also thrown them down the toilet. I have slept in abandoned buildings and stayed up all night, drinking cheap cider and smoking joints in an attempt to go to sleep with an empty stomach and a full head. I have carried knives and weapons due to the paranoia that followed me everywhere I went.

I have slept in a library with no place to call my own. I have hung around with wasters and deadbeats that I called my 'friends'. I have been robbed of my money and my possessions as I watched in fear and total powerlessness. I have had the urge to kill people in extreme frustration and pain as they screwed me over and took all that I owned. I have travelled from place to place just so I could sleep somewhere for the night. I have worn the same clothes for months and not washed them in weeks.

I have lost everything three times or more but each time much, much worse. I have had fridges filled with air and cupboards filled with nothing but crumbs from the last loaf of bread. I have sat there eating nothing but spoonfuls of peanut butter. Drinking black coffee as I can't even afford eighty pence for milk. I have been stood in my sister's garden with nothing but my boxers on, bleeding from my arms in a fit of rage and despair. I have felt the steel from the cuffs slapped around my boney wrists.

Kept in a cell over night as the officers wait for me to release my anger and sadness. I have bled from my body so many Goddamn times, the scars are there to prove that. I have looked in the mirror in disgust and self-loathing ideologies. I have lost all hope and gained all hate. I have regretted, wished and wanted in so many damn ways and means. I have laid there in sorrow, wishing I was never born. I have punched, kicked, damaged and broke myself down alongside my house countless times over.

I have been sat there with no friends, no girl of my own and nobody to bloody tell me everything will be fine. I have heard my stomach grumble more than times an angry dog. I have broken down and battered many family relationships. I have so very desperately needed help from those who I admire but I have hurt them numerous times so they've refused to help. I don't blame them but it is still bloody horrible to not have that support. I have begged for spliffs just so I can take my mind someplace else for a few hours.

I have gone weeks without money and had to carry my food parcels for miles just so I don't starve. I have experienced trench foot due to me walking for hours in the rain and snow, not just from ground working. I have slept on the floor in places that had dog shit everywhere. I have had to line up with the other homeless people just to get something to eat from the food truck that drove about in Bradford. I have seen people lighting up the foil and the spoon. I have seen holes in stomachs from where drugs have eaten away at them.

I have walked around with bloody blisters covering my feet as I try and find a place to stay. I have slept in hospital waiting rooms and been kicked out by security. I have curled up in a ball, hungry and sleepless. I have cried in absolute mental pain and torture, just praying that it will all end soon. I have had a phone on full battery but my contact list empty with nobody to call. I have sold my televisions, phones and computer games just so I could eat for the day.

I have never stolen money off of anyone but I have stolen weed and tobacco in an extremely, horrible and desperate attempt to take away some of the pain. I have made more mistakes than a dyslexic kid in school. I am that dyslexic kid by the way. I have walked around high as a kite wishing for a better life. I have sat down in the shower with my head in my hands, crying and screaming for someone to take away this pain. I have not slept or eaten in days due to stress, depression and inner torment.

I have scarred and bruised myself up many damn times in a self-destructive, chaotic warpath. I have been sitting in my flat with no carpets, blinds or heating. I have contemplated using heroin to numb the pain. I have punched myself in the face multiple times out of hate and uncontrollable anger. I have lost all hope in the blink of an eye and in return I have gained all hate and no trust. I have used drugs and alcohol daily to block out the intrusive thoughts. I have read many bloody debt letters that have built up against my name.

I have been lonely and solitary when things are at its toughest. I have had fifty pence on my gas meter to last for two weeks. I have sat in candlelight as the electric bill hasn't been paid. I have had cold showers when the gas has run out. I have been around criminals and drug addicts. I have been around evil and demonic people. I have witnessed evil acts and I have seen pain at its fullest. I have been sat in a graveyard with a stomach full of paracetamols and Polish beer, waiting to pass out and die.

I have been spat on, punched, slapped and broke down by the only girl I truly loved. I have had ashtrays, high heels and ornaments hit my head. I have given my last pound to a homeless man and I have been that homeless man. I have gone to church looking for guidance and redemption. I have been a law abiding citizen and I have been a petty criminal. I have broken the rules and I have followed them. I have had food bank parcels more times than I have bought a month's shopping.

I have battled with addictions and some I have lost and some I have won. I have laid outside wrapped in a foil blanket like a bloody baked potato. I have been screwed over more times than I have had sleepless nights. I have had leeches suck me dry of all my love, wealth and happiness. I have given away my last cigarette and I have given away my last fiver. I have been there for others but others haven't been there for me. I have been friends with the enemy. I have had no friends to call at night and I have had no girl to hold me tight.

I have wanted to die and I have wanted to live. I have walked miles just to be turned away. I have sat in the rain with nothing but a can of lager and a messed up mind. I have sat in the road hoping to be hit by a passer-by. I have grunted, groaned and given up many bloody times. I have lost the will to live and found it someplace else. I have sighed in pain and in relief. Oh god, I have really felt it all.

Chapter 6

I remember when me and Lauren were in Bradford one night, we had both been drinking. We were at this pub and Lauren was drinking her usual; two bottles of white wine. She had accompanied them with a shot of black Sambuca. Oh god it was vile! I had like one or two pints, I wasn't up to drinking that night. We had finished our drinks, then Lauren at this point was becoming an annoyingly rowdy bitch. I remember us both walking, well I was, Lauren was stumbling towards the McDonald's in Bradford. We had called in to buy a McChicken each.

We left the McDonald's and I remember seeing this group of six young chavs. Two lads and four girls. Lauren had started throwing up in the street and I remember one of them saying "Ew you damn rat" to Lauren. I just wanted to get back to the B&B we were staying at. I knew Lauren wasn't gonna leave it at that, she had said back to them "You're the bloody rat, piss off." She was pissed and every damn time she drank she became mouthy and violent. I knew they were younger than us, they were immature little arseholes.

I had just said to her "God's sake Lauren, just shut up and leave it." We walked off from outside the McDonald's, then took a right turn down the high street by Superdrug. It was raining quite badly so we had both gone underneath the doorway outside Superdrug to light a cig. I had sparked my cig then I remember looking up and seeing the same group of chavs walking towards us. I just thought 'For God's sake man, here we go.' They came over to us and started mouthing off trying to start a fight.

I remember Lauren stood in front of me trying to spark her fag when one of the girls had punched her straight in the nose. Lauren's nose went off to one side, it looked disfigured. She dropped to the floor, then all of a sudden blood started pissing out everywhere, all over my shoes. The four lasses had begun kicking the shit out of her and the two lads had begun punching me from either side. They tried to get me down to the floor but I just started whacking both of them as hard as I could.

I was outnumbered. Lauren had started to have a seizure and I remember her body jerking on the cold, rainy pavement. Blood pouring out of her nose and mixing with the rainwater, the girls were still kicking her as she lay unconscious. I thought 'They are gonna bloody kill her!' I dived onto the floor to cover Lauren's head with my body, I held her in my arms as my head collected the kicks and punches. I was getting kicked, punched and stamped on by six people.

A police officer came running up the high street shouting "Oi stop right there, get back here now!" The chavs scattered as me and Lauren lay in the pouring down rain. Cold, wet and filled with adrenaline. I was concussed whilst Lauren was unconscious. The copper had rang an ambulance as I was holding Lauren in my arms as she bled profusely. I explained to the copper what went on, then by that time the ambulance arrived. It took us both to Bradford Royal Infirmary. We got to the hospital then Lauren and I were taken in to see a nurse.

I wasn't arsed about me, I was more bothered about Lauren. I remember they'd put Lauren on a bed and gave her a drip to flush the alcohol out. They changed her damp, blood stained clothes for a hospital gown. I remember having to go for an MRI scan for my head to make sure there were no internal bleeding due to the kicks and punches it had just received. Luckily there was no damage, then they gave me two paracetamols for the concussion. I returned to Lauren's bedside, she was awake so I had asked her "Are you okay babe? How are you feeling?"

She had begun hurling abuse at me. I was so damn hurt as I had just taken a beating to protect her from further damage. I had been the one to stay by her side at that hospital bed. She even had a go at me for smoking a cigarette as I waited for her to come round. I honestly have never felt more alone and upset. She was the one attacking me this time. Her nose was crooked to one side, black eyes and purple bruising covered her face, legs and arms. She looked like a mess.

I remember her throwing up in one of those sick bowls they give you in hospital, black bile with tinges of blood filled the bowl. It didn't look healthy at all, time passed and I remember having to explain what happened to the police. I didn't know the attackers but what I did know is that I wanted to get the hell out of that place and into my bed back at the B&B. Hours passed by, me and Lauren had sobered up at this point. We were allowed to leave as there was no long term damage apart from Lauren's nose being slightly crooked to one side.

We jumped in a taxi and back to the B&B we went. We had both had a shower and dived into bed. "Oh thank God that is over" I said to Lauren. I remember for days after that event random people would stare at Lauren's black eyes and swollen nose then ask her "Are you alright love? Did he do this?" One person asked "Has he been beating you?" If only those people knew she was the abusive one. I remember this one dude who was in a car with his wife and kids outside the B&B. He shouted from his car window "You alright love, has he done that to your face?" He was properly staring me out with evil eyes, like he wanted to beat me up.

It was awful because every place we went, roughly two to three people would comment and ask her "Did he do that to you?" They would point at me and scowl as though I was the violent one, I have never hit Lauren, I have only restrained her when she has been throwing stuff at me. I have only pinned her down as she attempted to punch or kick me. She was the abusive one, she used to spit on me, kick me, punch me, nip me quite bloody hard, dig her nails into my arms and throw ornaments at me.

She was a violently evil person, I remember one time she had kicked me in the jaw whilst wearing high heels. It rocked my jaw, I remember feeling concussed, the high heel had split my jawline open and I began to bleed badly. The worst part of it was that nobody ever did anything. The police didn't do shit, her family didn't do shit. I couldn't do shit as I was too damn wrapped up in her twisted ways, I had to accept it like some bloody coward. I know I shouldn't have stayed with her but honestly by this point, I was too far in to easily return back.

I was too enthralled and too caught up in her manipulative and deceitful ways. I was a puppet on a string and she was the master of those strings. I remember this one time when I was staying at this hostel in Huddersfield. There was this guy who lived above me, it was around 4:00 AM and all of a sudden I heard this almighty crash. It woke me up and I shot out of bed, I looked outside and there was this fridge directly outside my window. I thought 'What the hell has just happened?'

I then saw a guitar get thrown out of the above window, the guy had started to throw everything out of his room and into the garden below. He had thrown his clothes, plates, cups and personal documents out the window. He had thrown out his bed covers and everything that was basically in his room.   He was proper on one, he had gone mental and must have
had a crisis or something because he was just muttering madness to himself. I could hear him shouting and bawling to himself, he also threw out his food. Packets of noodles were strewn about the garden below.

I remember the police coming to the hostel so I went to go check what was going on. He had barricaded himself in his room shouting "I'm gonna kill myself, I am gonna do it Goddamnit!" There were three coppers with tasers in their hands ready to fire. He had unlocked his door, then the coppers charged in and arrested him. He came out with no shoes or socks on, wearing a pair of jeans and a t-shirt. He didn't smell too good, it was like stale cider and sweat. His hair was matted with grease, his eyes were bloodshot and tearful and his glasses were partially broke as well.

The coppers escorted the guy down the stairs and out of the hostel. I had stood at the bottom of the stairs as they were leaving, he was just laughing at them and giggling to himself. I carried my half-asleep body back to bed, then fell into a deep sleep until the next day. Another time in that same hostel I remember when I had gone to use the shower, the bathroom and toilet were separate and were also communal. I walked in the damn bathroom and there was human shit all over the shower cubicle glass, it was smeared all over the door, all over the tiles and all over the glass.

It looked like someone had held their own shit in their hands and just painted a bloody picture with it all over the shower. Honestly I was so angry, I had never ever seen anything like it before. I felt grossed out because I always used that shower as it was directly opposite my room door. Another time I had been in that hostel there was this big African man who looked about twenty stone. I had got up quite early one day, I remember being stood in the communal kitchen at around 8:00 AM.

I was making some toast whilst sipping my first brew of the day. This African man had walked past the kitchen eating a whole joint of beef in a silver tray. Like a whole joint of beef to himself at bloody 8:00 AM. What the hell was he thinking? He had it in his hands, taking chunks off with his mouth. The whole hostel stunk of beef at 8:00 AM. He had no shoes, socks or t-shirt on, just a pair of grey, dirty, grime-covered jeans. It was like he had thrown meat juices all over himself. I have never been more confused in all my life.

I remember the time I was in a hostel in Bradford called Bradford Foyer. It was a right mad place to live, there were teenagers and adults mixed amongst one another. There were all kinds of characters knocking about. I remember when I was in there back in like 2018. I had never ever been in a hostel before, I didn't know what to expect. I remember my hostel room having nothing but a wardrobe, camp bed and a shower. We all had to share a kitchen, there were a few housing blocks next to each other.

The kitchen I had wasn't too bad apart from the bin bags were always full and were never emptied on time so mice started to appear. They called the different corridors 'clusters' as there were a few of us stopping in them at a time. I think there were around four others including myself living in one cluster. It went up to the next floor and there were also people below me as well. It was a huge hostel compared to the places I had been in after that one. There were blocks A, B and C that had three floors in each block.

The people I lived amongst weren't exactly sound people either. There was a girl who had moved in next door to me who was from Los Angeles. According to her that is where she came from. She had an American accent, she was a nice lass but had issues, I remember speaking to her and she was telling me "My mom called me a prostitute and that I have no respect for myself." I just looked at her in confusion, I mean what was I to say to that? She started to talk to me about her life, that she had come from America and that she didn't get along with her family at all.

She had basically told me snippets of her life, I think she was around eighteen. At that time I was nineteen. I guess she was a bit naive to the whole British way of life. She couldn't grasp certain things that I knew about. It wasn't her fault and I felt sorry for her as she was a nice girl but was left out from the others in the hostel. I remember someone had stolen her passport after she had let them in her room. She had things going missing all the time. There were these two criminal brothers at the hostel as well.

They had just come out of prison, one of them wasn't allowed to be the in the hostel so at times he snuck in. I remember I was knocking about the hostel one night and the American girl had been wandering on the next floor up from ours. Which was where the criminal brothers were. I was so confused as to why she was wandering upstairs. I went up and said "Hey what you up to?" She replied "Oh nothing just walking around whilst I wait for them two."

I was shocked because I didn't think she would wanna hang around with the two brothers due to the fact they were the total opposite of her. She wasn't overly shy or anything, she was quite talkative and upfront to be honest. I remember her going into the room of the two brothers. I was stood outside the cluster door thinking 'What the hell is going on in there?' I had nosily knocked on the door and asked for a cigarette. One of the brothers let me in and said "Yeah man no worries just come in for two."

I sat down on the chair by the window, I was given a cigarette by one of the brothers. I remember the American girl stood up against the wall by the bed. She was naked, like fully naked. She stood laughing as the two brothers sat there smoking a joint. I was so very confused as to why she was naked, I grabbed my cigarette and ran out the door in mad confusion. I said to all three of them "I guess I will head off then." I couldn't control my laughter. I found out later that night she had slept with them both.

I remember another time in that hostel, I had been selling some of my spare t-shirts and trousers that no longer fitted me. I sold them for tobacco, weed and a few quid here and there. I remember having this pair of Adidas Gazelles in a mint green colour, proper nice shoes they were. Anyways I had stupidly decided to swap them for another pair of Adidas shoes a lad also had. He chucked in a clump of baccy and a spliff with the pair he'd swapped me. They weren't bad looking shoes but wasn't in the best of conditions compared to my nice, green Gazelles.

I had to do what I had to do, I was broke and needed tobacco. It was a win-win situation when you have nothing. I remember when this guy had come down to my floor and opened the washing machine mid-cycle. He took all of my clothes out the washing machine, piss-wet through. He took them to his floor and placed them in his room, he was such an arsehole, nobody truly liked him. He had stolen some of my other clothing as well. Well what I had left anyway.

I remember one of the lads I was knocking about with going up to his room and booting his door wide open. I grabbed my piss-wet through clothes, then took them back down to my kitchen. The guy wasn't in of course, he had gone out somewhere. One day I got back to the hostel, walked into my room and saw this little mouse peek its head round the corner. It looked at me for like two minutes then ran off down the back of my wardrobe. I remember saying to myself "Oh God sake, of course there's a mouse in my room."

The mouse had chewed through my clothes in the wardrobe. It had chewed through my food bank supplies that were on my table. There were holes in almost every item of clothing from where the mouse had chewed at them. There were grains of rice and porridge dotted around the room as well. The mouse had ravaged my food and clothes whilst living behind my wardrobe. The reason there were mice is because of the filthy bastards living around me. Their rooms cluttered and stinking.

Full of empty takeaway boxes and food wrappers. The bins in the kitchen were full of all kinds of waste. Full to the brim and smelling like rotting shite. It was awful, I felt as though the mouse had a higher level of hygiene than those people I lived amongst. I remember one time in that hostel, I had been knocking about with this guy, he was alright. He wasn't a prick or anything but I knew not to trust him. Me and him was about to leave the hostel, I had a Fray Bentos pie in a can. Chicken and mushroom it was, I had mushy peas to go with it as well.

I had the pie and peas in my hand because I was gonna cook them in the other kitchen across from my cluster. We were leaving so I had decided to put the pie and peas away until later on. The guy said to me "Oh you can keep your food in my room until we get back if you want?" My room was in a different block and I couldn't be arsed taking it all the way back. I agreed and stored my pie and peas in this guy's room. We went out into Bradford city centre and met some more people from the hostel.

Time went by and I had totally forgotten that I left my pie and peas in his room. I got back to the hostel and I knocked on his door as he had gone back before me, I asked "Can I grab my pie and peas mate?" I was bloody starving as I hadn't eaten anything all day. I was dying for something filling and warm. He turned around and said to me "Oh sorry mate I have eaten them." I was so damn pissed off, I literally was struggling for food as well and the dude goes and eats my bloody tea?!

Oh God man, I have been around vermin. I just said to him "For God sake mate, that was all I had, why would you steal my food?" I honestly have never stolen someone's food, that is bang out of order, that is basically someone's lifeline, they need it to bloody breathe. I also remember the time Lauren had come over to hostel to see me. We were in my room when Lauren had begun going crazy at me… as always. We started to argue about our relationship and possibly ending it.

I had said to her "I can't carry on with your abuse and your constant drinking." She had replied "Oh piss off, I don't care no more, I am all you have anyway." I just said to her "Look, you're gonna have to leave because I am not getting kicked out as you are shouting too loud and staff will hear you." She had then picked up a full jar of pasta sauce, opened it and then threw the contents all over my room. In a circular motion so my curtains, bedding and walls were splattered with tomato and herb sauce.

She then threw the jar against the wall and it smashed into a million pieces. Lauren then walked out in a pissed-up state and left me to scrub the walls for the next hour or two. I had honestly endured enough at this point. I remember when Lauren had the abortion of our unborn child back in 2018. I was shitting myself as I had never planned to have a child of my own. She had told me a couple months prior to the abortion that she couldn't get pregnant as she was on the implant. I wasn't ready at all, neither was she.

She was mentally unstable and so was I. She had an alcohol problem and I was still living freely enjoying my life but I had major issues myself at that time. I was on medication, smoking weed and living a hectic party life every day. Yeah I know it probably ain't the best of combo's to do but I have lived and I have learnt many awful lessons. I remember the morning me and Lauren went to Doncaster to get the abortion done. I was in a hostel in Huddersfield, the same hostel where that deranged person smeared their shit all in the shower.

I remember having to sneak Lauren in the through my bedroom window as it was on a ground floor. I had metal shuttering that you could open with a key. I always kept the shuttering unlocked as I used to sneak round the back of the hostel at night and creep through my window like the night stalker. I sneaked Lauren in because we had to go to Doncaster the next day to the abortion clinic. We had to call at Leeds train station first to switch trains. It was the morning of the abortion, it was around 5:00 AM on a cold and frosty winter day.

We woke up in my single bed, I had made us both a brew as I had a kettle in my room. The hostel room came with an ashtray which was blessed. We had our morning brews with a sterling fag. My eyes were stuck together with sleep, oh I could've done with more. We got ourselves ready and left the building for Huddersfield train station. It was 5:40 AM at this point. I only lived like ten minutes from the station so it was an easy walk. We got to the train station and smoked another cig outside on the steps.

It was bloody freezing and I just wanted this day to end. We had jumped on a train and headed for Leeds. It took about forty-five minutes to get there. I remember being sat in the train carriage looking out at the morning sky. It had this grey and blue tinge. Black birds followed the trains passing by as the intercom woman announced "Next stop Dewsbury." I didn't know what to expect as I hadn't been in such an awful position before. I remember each station the train stopped at gave us both a saddening reminder of the depressingly harsh truth of what was to come.

Looking back now I am glad we didn't have the child as I know my life would've been a living hell. What chance would the poor bastard have had? A violent, alcoholic mother and a mentally unstable father. I wasn't ready and neither was Lauren. The train got to Leeds so it was now time to switch trains, we wandered off to board the Doncaster train. I remember being sat on the Doncaster train, watching the other trains leaving the station thinking 'Oh the freedom to go wherever one wishes.'

I have always loved the idea of jumping on a train, going someplace totally new and refreshing. I hate staying in one place for such a long time, I need the excitement of something brand new. Me and Lauren were as silent as the night, we didn't say much as I think we were both feeling guilty deep down. The train then started up, the engine rumbled. The vibrations from the engine coursed through the window and into my head as I leant against the glass. This is it, no turning back.

I can't quite remember the journey to Doncaster but I know I had never been before. I hadn't any reason to. I was still half-asleep, my stomach growled with hunger. It took a few hours to get there but once we did, we carried ourselves off of the train and down the platform. I remember getting to the train station exit and instantly lighting up a fag. Oh the feel of nicotine powering through my system. The only comfort that day was sterling tobacco. We had walked to the abortion clinic through the city centre.

By this time it was still early morning, I remember walking past a group of workmen. They just eyed Lauren up, I didn't have the energy to respond with the words "I am her boyfriend you know." I was used to cars beeping their horns at and guys blurting out sexual comments as they she walks by. I always felt like she was never my girl. She loved the groping eyes and the cheeky comments that filled her mind. We got to the clinic and Lauren spoke to the receptionist. They asked us to pass into the waiting room with all the other guilt-ridden couples.

There were women crying and boyfriends biting the skin from around their fingernails. It was saddening to see all those people who were in the same boat as us, just in different circumstances and lifestyles. I remember I sat there reading through a gossip magazine as there was nothing else to do. I didn't have data to browse the internet or use Instagram so I had to sit there and read about the pointless lives of celebrities.

I remember reading this story about this woman whose dad had died through him having a heart attack at the wheel of his car and crashing it. There was a psychic medium who was talking to the woman whose dad it was. She was saying "Your father has come through in spirit and is telling you be careful of this person and watch out for this happening." It was interesting to read as I have always believed there is another world, a better world than this one. I have always believed in spirits and the afterlife.

I mean there has to be, all those people can't be wrong can they? It would be lovely to know that we are guided and protected by the other side. It would also be lovely to know that all our loved ones are elsewhere. Happier and healthier away from the pains of this world. Lauren was sat messaging her friend. I on the other hand couldn't message anyone as there was no friend for me to talk to. I have never had a best friend before, only acquaintances who dossed about with me or chatted to me because they had nobody else and I had something they wanted.

I remember Lauren being called in to see a nurse who then gave her a tablet that basically induced her into labour, but in reality it just got her body ready for the abortion process. She came out looking sleepless and weak, she sat down and started crying in pain, both physical and mental. She was leaning over her knees clutching her stomach in agony. I was stroking her hair, comforting her with words such as "Everything is gonna be fine soon, I am here for you no matter what." I didn't know what else to do but try my best to give her my love and compassion.

I had never endured such a saddening experience before. I was sat there both in relief and guilt as I never wanted to get Lauren pregnant. It was purely an accident as when she came off the implant we hadn't been careful enough. I remember we'd been on a break for a few months and I had received a text that read 'I am pregnant and I think it is your child'. Obviously this is Lauren we are talking about and that girl always loved male attention, I mean she cheated on me later that year so how was I to know it was mine?

Deep down I didn't want the child as like I said we were both far from ready and incapable of looking after the child. The nurse called Lauren in for the operation, I wasn't allowed in so I had to wait in the seating area for over five hours on my own. I don't know why it took so long but it felt like forever. I remember ripping bits of paper up then turning them into paper balls. I sat throwing them into the waste bin in front of me. I went outside for numerous cigarettes, I felt so alone in that situation.

I couldn't phone my family as I didn't want them to think bad of me and bombard me with questions and lectures. I had no friend to comfort me and tell me "Don't worry mate we will have a chat when you're back in Hudds." I was already going through my own shit with my mental health and housing situation. My mind was flooded with grief, pain and torment, this was just the icing on the cake. I had nothing else to do but sit, wonder and wait until Lauren finally crept out the operation room and greeted me with the words "It is done, that is it now, let's go home."

Her face was emotionless and weathered. I remember thinking 'Oh man this is messed up, how can life be like this?' Lauren came outside with me and we had shared a cigarette, she then said to me "I don't know why you are so bothered, it isn't that much of a big deal." I literally screamed at her "How awful Lauren, how can you say such a cruel thing?" I was actually heartbroken that she could be so cold and dark. We had got our stuff together then headed back to Doncaster train station.

On the way back to the station we stopped off at Burger King. I got a Chicken Royale with fries and a Coca-Cola as my beverage. We wandered through the shopping centre and flooded back out onto the streets. I remember seeing this homeless man and I had given him a cigarette then said "Sorry I can't give you money mate but here take this." I proceeded to hand him the cig. His face lit up with joy, I felt comforted for the first time that day.

We got back to the train station then hopped on a train back to Leeds. We got back to Leeds train station, then jumped on a Huddersfield train. We finally got back to my hostel, the day was over and so was my dread. I have felt guilty ever since as I remember Lauren going to the toilet in my hostel and she had left the abortion operation letter on my dresser. It had full details of the operation. The dates and all the information on the procedure, it said how many weeks she was pregnant.

The letter said '20 weeks' which basically meant she was five months pregnant before the abortion. The poor thing was partially developed and would have had a gender. I felt even guiltier as the child was a mistake and didn't ask for any of this shit. Looking back now I am so bloody glad I didn't have one with that evil bastard, the funny thing is, she now has a child with the man she cheated on me with. Both of them are not right in the head and that poor child will be a product of an intoxicated night of madness, not planned and not wanted.

I am just glad she isn't with me no more. She is now a problem for somebody else, I have never wanted kids of my own if I am honest. I don't have the time for them in the nicest way possible, I just love being free and able to do whatever I like when I like. I have no ties of any kind so I can do as I please. Remember earlier on when I said oh the freedom to go wherever one wishes? I can do that now as I am free and single.

I remember living in Edgerton Hotel in Huddersfield, I was living there because I was homeless and had no other home. The council placed me there. I had been living there for a few months in this shoebox of a room. Lonely, depressed and broke. I was living off of the free breakfasts they gave us every morning and had to steal food during the day to get my meals in. I was stealing sandwiches, crisps, chocolate bars and drinks from the Sainsbury's in town. I had lost so much weight and was surely malnourished.

I was living next to this addict who was extremely strange and horrible. He used to wake me up every morning rambling to himself whilst pouring his vomit down the toilet in a plastic jug. I could smell crack smoke lingering from underneath his door. It was awful, he would stay up all hours and use drugs in his room. He also injected heroin frequently as I was soon to find out. One night I remember coming back from being out in town. He had knocked on his wall to alert me to come to his room.

He shouted "Oi you next door, come here a sec." I was anxiously on edge but went next door anyway. I knocked on his door then he opened it slightly. He was sat on his bed with a curtain tie around his neck, felt tip marker drawn all over his arms. He had wrote ramblings all over himself, I was so damn confused as to why he had done this. I looked down onto his dresser and saw empty syringes that were used for heroin. They were dirty and had residue still in them. His room was filled with smoke of some kind and he smelt like he'd been decomposing for months on end.

He said to me "Have you got anything for me?" I replied "What do you mean?" He then said "Do you have any weed or drugs for me?" I hadn't even a spliff for myself never mind him, I said to him "Nah mate I ain't got anything at all." He then started to raise his voice and become irritated with withdrawal symptoms.

He blurted out in a drugged up voice "We are gonna have a problem then aren't we? Give me some bloody drugs now! You better give me something!" I had become quite angry and on edge so I said "Piss off and leave me alone! I don't owe you anything!"

He stood up as though he was gonna do something which by that time the receptionist lady had come down the hallway to see what the noise was about. She said to us both "What is going on here? You can't be shouting in here, we have other guests." I told her "He had just started banging on my wall and asking me for drugs, saying if I didn't give him any he would hurt me." She told him "Leave this young man alone and stay in your room, stop bothering people." He had become quite angry then started shouting all kinds of abuse at me and the receptionist.

I was stood there in total confusion and rage, he then said to me "I know what you are, you're a rapist. You're a rapist and you are bad." I was quite pissed off at this point as I have never, ever done anything of the sort. I certainly am not a rapist. I have never been to jail before and I defo aren't planning to either. In a fit of rage I booted him up his arse with my steel toe boots on. I booted him as hard as I could then he flew onto his bed. The receptionist had said "Woah, woah take it outside please, we can't be having that in here."

I replied "I am sorry love but I ain't having that, I ain't having him saying shit like that to me." He unsteadily got off his bed and said "Come on then, meet me round the back of the hotel in two minutes." I agreed and said "Alright give me a minute and I'll come round the back." I powered off outside and down the black metal steps behind the hotel. There was this youngish lad having a cig outside his room at the bottom of these steps.

He had said "Alright mate, how you doing?" I hadn't seen him before but I was friendly and replied "Yeah I'm alright pal thanks, this crackhead next door to me has just started going off on one threatening me to come outside so I've come out to fight him." The lad replied "Are you? Where is he? Where are you off to fight him?" I asked him to come with me so I could show him who I was talking about. The addict had finally come outside and round the back of the hotel. We got out the view of cameras and stood on this patch of grass like a minute walk from the back of the hotel.

It was straight across from Edgerton Cemetery, the addict had stood in front of me and the young lad was stood to the right of us both. The young lad was saying "What is this all about then? Why are you both going to fight?" I had explained what had gone on and what was said in the hotel. The addict was blurting out nothing but muddled up sentences. The young lad was just laughing at this whole situation and so was I to be honest. I had been stood there for around ten minutes when the addict pulled out a pillowcase that held a thick piece of plastic and a dirty heroin needle.

He was actually gonna stab me with it, he held it within his hand and was ready to drive it into me. Bloody horrible bastard, how sick can you be? You would stab someone with a dirty needle then mess up their life up over a drugged induced dispute? I had turned around to look for a brick, I was ready for anything at this point. I couldn't find a brick and I certainly wasn't gonna fight a man who had a dirty needle in his hand.

The young lad said to him "Woah mate you can't be doing that, you can't be pulling shit like that out on people." The horrible addict replied "Yeah but look at him, he would beat my head in, I ain't letting him do that. I haven't got a chance with my leg." He had a bad leg and couldn't walk properly. We had been standing arguing for like half an hour-ish, I had seen somebody come over from the side of the hotel. It was the receptionist woman, she said "If you don't pack it in, I am calling the police and they can sort it out."

I was in no mood to be arrested that night and I defo wasn't gonna get arrested over some low-life smackhead like him. I had walked fast out of the situation and back into my hotel room where I was safe and warm. I sat down on my bed and I just shook my head in disbelief, I truly couldn't believe what had just gone on and how close I was to having a life-changing experience. I have never trusted people like that as one minute you are talking to them and the next you are on the floor with a needle in your eye, crying for help because you know you ain't gonna be right again.

I have never been a fighter in life, I have never gone out my way to cause shit or start fights. I just don't agree with violence as it never ever solves anything. Violence just breeds more violence, you hurt someone, they hurt you. You hurt them badly, then they do something much worse. It is a never ending cycle of shite, I have never seen anything good come from violence. It is like gang violence for example, one gang member stabs another, then that gang member shoots that guy, then that guy kills him and so on.

I am a lover not a fighter, I have had to stop people from stabbing others as they hold out their knives in rage. I have seen people get chased down with knifes. I have seen gangs charge at innocent people, kick and punch them to the ground, five people on one. Beating their heads into the cold concrete and blood covering the streets. I have seen people crying in fear as they get jumped on and punched repeatedly until they are unconscious. I have seen bottles get thrown at people and bricks used as weapons.

I remember in Bradford one time I was with a group of people, chilling out drinking in a park. It was when I was in Bradford Foyer. Anyways me and these people were chilling when a group of chavs had charged at us all, then spread out and began battering everyone they came into contact with. For some unknown reason they didn't touch me at all, I remember one of themsaying "Yo you got a cig?" I had nervously given him one, then he ran off away from me.

The aftermath of it all was madness, some of the people I was with were on the floor rolling about, bleeding from their noses and mouths. Bust lips and damaged noses, heads that had been kicked and stamped on through nothing but mindless violence. This one guy who was with my group had recently undergone brain surgery as he sadly suffered with a brain tumor due to being hit by a car. I remember seeing him sat on this bench being booted in his head by about six other people.

He was shouting in pain "I have just had brain surgery, please stop it! Please stop, I haven't done anything wrong." I was totally in shock as I have never witnessed that level of cruelty before and in such a full view of it as well. There was blood from various people pooled around the benches and bloodied footprints leading off into the night. The chavs had sprinted off into the dark landscape, all that was left were unconscious and crying beings. Laid on the floor in agony from the array of violence dished out to them.

Still to this day I wonder why I was never attacked, it was like something from a film. I was stood in this crowd of people, smoking a cigarette with a three hundred and sixty degree view of just pure violence and madness. I was expecting somebody to punch me or kick me down to the ground but honestly there was no pain given to me. The only interaction I had was with one of the chavs who'd asked "Yo you got a cig?" He had a skeleton mask on, wearing a red and black jacket, black trainers and trackies.

I couldn't see his face only hear his voice. I was quite drunk at this point as I had been sharing a bottle of cider with one of the people who got attacked. I used to spend a lot of time in this park, drinking being a rebel without a cause. Our souls are our life force, our bodies nothing more than mortal vehicles in this saddening world. Oh it goes to show that life is certainly a box of chocolates... you never know what you're gonna get.

Chapter 7

I remember when I had swam across the Lake District back in 2018. I had never been to the lakes before, it was such a refreshing experience. I remember having bleached red hair... I have no clue what I was thinking but I have these moments where I change my whole look. I don't know but maybe that is why I can shapeshift into different subcultures. Anyways, I had swam across the Lake District for the very first time. It was mad because I could have seized up and drowned, to be honest nobody was close enough to rescue me as the only people in the lake were me and Lauren but she was in a kayak near the land.

I on the other hand was in the middle of a lake that was about as deep as six houses stacked on one another. I could have drowned and that'd been it but luckily I survived it, honestly my muscles didn't thank me for it. I remember swimming for like half an hour straight, it could have been more but I can't truly remember. I had managed to get across the lake, then half-way back. I had to hoist myself into the kayak on the way back as I had Lauren bring it to me in case I seized up.

I didn't know that I could have seized up until I got back onto land and had spoken to Lauren's dad about it. I was quite amazed actually as I had never been much of a swimmer. Only time I went swimming was at Barnsley Metrodome where I would pencil dive right into the water. It is crazy how ballsy I was as a kid as now I would be shitting it on the top diving board. I suppose as a kid though you don't feel fear and you defo don't see it properly compared to an adult.

I love camping at the lakes though as I have always cherished being out in nature. It was summer 2018 and the weather felt euphoric. Sat around the campfire under the starry night, drinking a can of lager with a cigarette. Just soaking in the universal beauty of the night. Oh it was lovely to have the campfire burning beautifully, illuminating the faces of those sitting around it. Hearing the innocently drunk conversations of the people close by. The crackle and the pop of the firewood ablaze.

Oh it was so very wonderful to be around all the mushy pea coloured trees and the naturistic values that have been here long before us. I slept in a huge six-man tent in my own little section within a toasty and warm sleeping bag. I remember waking up each morning, having a cup of coffee brewed in a vintage camping ketal on a gas powered stove. I felt like I was surely in a different world being at the lakes, it was so thrilling to smell the natural air and the still-burning firewood from the night before.

To hear the sweet tones of the birds above and the laughter of others as they play in the water. It was so delightful to feel the earthy grass and mud beneath my feet, entwining around my toes as I walked around the campsite. It was truly comforting and scrumptious to taste the runny fried eggs with the smoked crispy bacon flavours as they danced around my mouth. Oh I felt at peace, so very free and young. I truly do love going there, I haven't been in such a long, long time.

I know that one day I shall return in higher spirits than before. For I know each time I go, my love for the lakes grows stronger and deeper every single time. I love the desolate surroundings, the tranquil array of silence that flows throughout the morning and evening. I remember me, Lauren and her family had gone for breakfast at one of the local cafes. I had a full English breakfast of course. The meal included these absolutely delicious buttered mushrooms, nicely grilled tomatoes, succulent and rich sausages, smoked crispy bacon, bright yellow runny eggs and slightly burnt but golden toast.

I had a medium-sized coffee to help wash it down and honestly it was like all the flavours were making love then spawning more and more flavour in each filling bite I took. I seriously adore such delights, I am such a food lover, I love all kinds of foods. From Jamaican to Mexican to Spanish to Italian to Chinese and to American. I admire each country's desired dishes and comfort foods. I remember when we had first got to the Lake District, I had been down at the lake near the water with Lauren.

I said to her "Dare me to go in with all my clothes on?" The water was defo in a minus temperature as there wasn't any sun at this point. It was later in the evening and the sun had already set. Me being me I wanted to prove myself so I ran straight into the icy cold water and dived right under it. Oh wow, the frozen shock of the water had rattled through my bones and into my soul. I didn't expect it to be that cold, my clothes had been soaked piss-wet through which made it even worse as they were heavier due to the water sponged within the fibers.

I remember gasping for my breath as I felt an instant unexpected blow from the shock that had been delivered to me. It was like being blasted in the face by a hundred-miles-per-hour fire hose filled with minus eighty degrees water. I remember swimming in the lake for about ten minutes, I had to charge straight out the water then back onto dry land. I remember walking back to the campsite, soaked and shivering with hyperthermia. My teeth chattering with the same sound as somebody's finger rapidly clicking backspace on a keyboard.

I could've chewed a hole in an oak table by the speed my jaw was going. I wandered back to the campsite, stripped off and laid curled up in a towel within my sleeping bag. I was delightfully warm and cozy by then. I had sparked a fag up and made myself a heavenly creamy hot chocolate, with a handful of marshmallows. I was in a dreamlike state at this point. I felt at peace with myself and the world, for once in such

127

a long while I had nothing on my mind. I sat peeking out the tent entrance, savoring the flavours of my sterling cigarette and my lukewarm hot chocolate.

What more could one possibly want in such a moment? I was euphorically safe and sound. If you get two people and ask them to look outside of a window, those two people will have a completely different point of view and have a totally different vision in mind. That it is how we perceive our own lives, we can either look at the negatives or we can look for the positives that aren't clearly seen. We must change our point of view to see what truly matters and what truly gives us happiness.

I remember when I walked seven miles just to see Lauren. I had been living in Bradford Foyer and that place was proper getting to me, I had mice eating my clothes and I had people eating what little food I had left. I felt trapped in a prison of chaos, sleepless nights and starvation, I had criminals and soon-to-be convicts surrounding my every move. Knife marks dotted into the fire-proof doors, the late night parties almost every day. I know this place wasn't for me, it truly wasn't right.

Robbing food from Lidl as my heart and mind was playing piggy in the middle. I was losing hope for something bright but oh those days were suffocating me ever so tightly. Standing on the red bridge on Manningham Lane, smoking joint after joint, the haze hitting my brain. Walking miles in the pissing down rain, oh dear universe please don't make me the same. I don't fit in with these people, they are truly lame. I had walked seven miles one day all the way from Bradford city centre to Riddlesden.

I thought it would have done me the world of good but oh once I got there I was left out in the mud. I remember walking in my Adidas Stan Smiths that I had found outside a charity shop drop off point in

Bingley. They were fake of course, my previous shoes were flapping more than a scared wannabe. I had my bleach blonde hair, extremely unkempt and riddled with excess Brylcreem. I had no money nor did I have tobacco, I had nobody to call on my Nokia 3310. I was in a battle with life and oh life was truly winning, I had seen days, weeks and months of pure sinning.

I walked through Bingley and looked at the normal young couples and wished for something alike. The pain she had caused me was like my heart on a spike. I had wandered for about three and a half hours, expecting and hoping that Lauren be at home to welcome me with open arms. I had got to her parent's house then I remember Lauren and her mother pulling up in the driveway in their beetroot coloured BMW. I was sleepless, starved and desperate for compassion. Lauren got out of the car holding in her hand a freshly made Maccies with Pepsi to wash down the unhealthily delicious meal.

My mouth was watering in temptation and absolute hunger. I said to her "I have just walked seven miles to see you, please can I come in? I need a drink or something." She replied "What are you doing here? You shouldn't be here." I was honestly so devastated I couldn't have a single brew to just get my bearings and to rest my aching skeleton. She wouldn't allow me in the house even though we were together and apparently we were totally fine at this point. Oh my back was killing, she never did have the time for me.

I always got the latter end of things, it was far from sweet, all I did was wander the streets until I could hear my own rapid heartbeat. I wasn't allowed in the house and was turned away. I was gasping for a cig when I kindly asked her "Please can I have a cig Lauren?" She had replied "No I am not giving you anything, they are mine." I truly felt like I had come into contact with an ice queen. I just wanted to wake up from this hellish dream. I started to become frustrated and began to scream.

She stood in front of me eating her juicy and filling Big Mac whilst I stood in pain with an aching back. I honestly felt as though I was around a stranger, she didn't even hug or kiss me. I was stuck in this isolated nightmare, I was pulling on my hair desperately wanting to sit with her on the garden chairs. I used to sit in her parent's garden, looking up at the night sky as my sterling cigarette burned brighter than the moon. I wasn't ever a part of her, in her cold heart there wasn't much room.

I missed the comfort of my mother's cooking and our conversations that went on for hours. This wasn't my home, at Lauren's parents'. I was far from home, I craved that innocent life I used to lead but now it had changed and oh my mother's heart used to bleed. I had asked Lauren again for a cigarette and finally she agreed to chuck me a cig. She told me "If I give you a cig will you go away?" I honestly felt like cement had filled up her heart and she was soulless with no compassion. I had always done anything and everything for her.

I truly did all I could. I remember once I robbed her a pair of high heels, only for months later those same heels had cracked my jaw out of her drunken wickedness. I risked life and limb just to keep her mine, she risked dinting her ego and becoming human all for her own gain. She was so egotistical and all for herself. I was holding onto her whilst risking my health as she placed me on the higher shelf. I had lit my sterling cigarette and began walking down her dark, lonely and icy street.

So alone I could only hear my own feet patrolling the concrete. I had wandered down to Bingley train station with a last hope of skipping a train back to Bradford city centre. I managed to get on a train and skip it to a stop just outside of the city centre as I was far too tired to walk. I hadn't eaten anything all bloody day, I was losing weight faster than a Holocaust victim. I remember

I had been kicked off the train just before the city centre by a dickhead conductor. I was hiding in the toilet thinking 'Great, I can just stay in here till I get back to the city centre.'

Unluckily for me there was a person asking to use the toilet. I didn't want the poor sod to piss themselves so I walked out the toilet. Head down and hoping I wouldn't be caught but I was caught like a deer in headlights. The conductor stood with his ticket machine in hand, looking at me with those 'you got a ticket eyes'. I know he was just doing his job but honestly I told him "Look mate I am broke and need to get back to my hostel to eat some food as I haven't eaten all day." He replied "Get off the train or I am calling the police to come arrest you."

I was filled with rage as I was only a stop or two away from the city centre. I had been kicked off so I waited for the next train at a different station about twenty mins away. I remember being outside the station I got kicked off at, I had gone outside to try and pinch a cig whilst I waited for the next train. I had looked down and there I saw a partially rusted switchblade. I had picked it up out of confusion. I gave it a quick look, then I saw a police van roll by and I became paranoid. I threw it into a set of bushes nearby.

I had waited around half an hour or so for the next train. I got on and felt blessed I didn't have to walk back in the dark as I was in Bradford after all. I was stood up by the doors of the train, clutching the handrail in nail biting anxiety. I really didn't wanna be caught again, I especially didn't wanna be fined or arrested. I managed to get to Bradford Foster Square station but oh how silly was I. I forgot that there were barriers and conductors waiting for me once I pulled in.

I had slowly but surely got off the platform, then wandered over to the barriers. I was greeted by a conductor but he wasn't an arsehole like the last. I had told him "I am waiting for my friend to transfer me some money to pay for a ticket." He said "No worries mate let me know when you have got the money so I can let you through." No friend was transferring me money, I had no friends after all. I especially didn't have any money, time passed and it had roughly been around twenty mins or so.

I remember pretending to ring my 'friend' and chase them up about transferring me my train fare. I stood there talking to absolutely nobody. I was holding my Nokia 3310, I had to just make up chat. "Hiya mate when are you transferring my train fare? I need that train fare man, the conductor is waiting for me." I felt like a right idiot, I was talking to a dead phone. I remember the conductor saying to me "It is alright mate, I will let you through this once but not again." I had sighed in relief then walked through the barriers feeling accomplished.

I had wandered back through the streets of Bradford city centre then all the way up Manningham Lane. I also remember one extremely frosty, steel cold night when I was walking down Manningham Lane by myself. I had seen a cat that was frozen laying down as though it was sleeping and had been set in stone. It was a purely frozen, poor little thing. I had never seen a rigor mortis-like cat before, sounds funny I know. Anyways I had got back to Bradford Foyer, whacked off my clothes and switched on the shower.

I remember sitting down in the shower, feeling the only warmth I had felt all bloody day. I had no bodily warmth from my 'girlfriend' and I had no warmth from my clothes either. The shower cubicle was my only way of comfort that night, I had nobody to hold me nor did I have anybody to talk with. It was just me, my thoughts and the scalding hot shower. I still sit in the shower and absorb every bit of comfort I gain from the water, the warmth of it brings me a sense of protection and hope that I will be one day warm again. In the arms of an angel who adores me.

I remember when I used to do groundworks, I would get up at 6:00 AM and have a morning cigarette with a deliciously made brew. I would throw on my work overalls and steel toe boots. Back pack on and out the door I would go. I would leave the house for around 6:45 AM and head down to the main road at the bottom of Honely Centre, then wait on the main road for my lift to work from my boss's brother. I would work from Monday to Friday, sometimes Saturdays and do around fifty-four hours a week.

It was such a hugely tiring job as I had to be up extremely early, able to lift heavy equipment, metal shuttering and tools. I had to be on the ball with things as I had to measure wood, steel and rebar which then would be used for more important jobs such as building houses and foundations. You couldn't get the measurements wrong as this could jeopardize further work being done. I had to be on point with my work as it was all about the finished result. It had to look spot on, how we would want our own property.

I used to saw wooden beams down into smaller ones that would be used as a parameter around the foundations. I had to use steel saws to shorten rebar down which were then used for the actual foundations of the property. Concrete would then be poured on top of the rebar to then build a solid wall. I remember being waist high in concrete one day, I had to use a spazzle to even out the freshly poured concrete. It was like smoothing out the icing on a cake, it was so satisfying.

I had worked there for around seven or eight months, another reason I couldn't mess up is because I was the new lad and I didn't wanna lose my job so soon. I wanted

133

to prove to my work mates and my bosses that I was made for the job, I remember when I was working in my uncle's builders yard I mentioned earlier, I was leveling out some uneven ground for the owner of the storage facility as he had asked me to do the job. He mentioned that I would be paid well. I remember having to dig up all the old mud and tarmac using a pickaxe and shovel.

I had never done such work before. It was summertime and red hot, I was sweating profusely and drinking water every minute. I had to also unblock the storage facility drains by climbing down a grate then using a wooden rod to probe the mud, gravel and grass that had been stuck in the drain pipes underground. It was a messy job, luckily though it wasn't a toilet drain as I would've been knee deep in shit and piss. I remember standing down the drain with my head popping out above like I was in some trench from World War Two.

I spent like forty minutes clearing the blocked drain, stood in muddy water and gravel that filled my boots slightly. I had trench foot whilst being at my ground working job. I remember taking off my boots one day after work and it smelt awful, my feet were a yellowy white colour with a layer of dead skin. I honestly thought I was gonna lose my feet or something. I had finished unblocking the drains then I resumed my other job of leveling out the uneven ground above me.

I climbed out and began to smash the broken tarmac into even smaller bits. I was doing this whole job on my own as before I was giving my uncle a hand doing some odd jobs around his yard. I had left him to carry on doing his jobs to do my own work for the owner of the lot. I was shoveling the piles of old mud and dead weeds into the bucket for a digger, then the owner of the facility had taken it away. I had then grouped all the odd bits of broken tarmac together which were thrown into the bucket for the digger nearby.

I had successfully leveled the ground out and tidied

up quickly and efficiently. The owner of the lot had said "You've done an excellent job mate, here's your money." He handed me like sixty-five quid for about an hour and a half's work. I felt so blessed I had earned this money through hard work, sweat and back pain. I remember one day I was at my ground working job, I had been standing on top of some metal shuttering. Metal shuttering is basically the mould for concrete as it is being poured into the gaps at the top of the shuttering.

The shuttering holds the wet concrete in place overnight and is then removed once the concrete inside of it is dry. It is like pouring water into an ice cube mould, you leave it in the freezer for a couple of hours then it is solid ice. That is what metal shuttering did for concrete, it acted as a mould so that the concrete would then dry hard like steel. Once the shuttering was off, you'd be left with a concrete wall that went around the parameter of the foundations. It was so fascinating to see how houses and other buildings are made.

That is why growing up I had always loved the TV series *How It's Made*. Anyways, I was standing on top of the metal shuttering and it was time to pack up our tools and head home. I had been holding a power drill in my arms, the ones that need a generator. I had stupidly decided to jump from the shuttering and over a seven foot trench below me. I was so close to landing the jump on the overside, it was like a few feet in front of me. I had tried to land on the dirt at the overside of the shuttering but I had fallen down the trench below.

I had thrown the power drill in the spot where I should've landed. I had slipped down this trench and thankfully there was rebar poking out the shuttering. The rebar was used for holding the shuttering together when concrete would be poured into the holes at the top. It was so bloody lucky that the rebar was there as I had grabbed hold of it to stop myself from falling further down the trench and possibly breaking a bone. I remember gripping the rebar with fear. Bearing in mind the rebar could have gone through my head or my body but thank God it didn't.

I was truly being watched over that day as it could've been my last day ever. I have always been a grafter, I may not have stayed within jobs for long but that is because I truly get bored so easily with things. I have had many jobs throughout life but I deeply do not like working dead-end jobs that ain't going anywhere. My first job was in a clothes shop called BANK Fashion. I had recently left school so I was around sixteen at the time. My brother had gotten me the job as he knew one of the lasses that worked there as a manager.

I had worked there as a store assistant, stocking the shelves with clothes, shoes and accessories. It was my first proper job, I worked there for around four months until I left one lunchtime and never returned. I remember working there a few days a week. It was a part-time job that was truly soul destroying. I never enjoyed it fully as I felt I was just a skivvy to the rest of the older workers there. I remember having to mop and vac the shop floor every day when it was closing time.

I wasn't supposed to do the cleaning all the time but like I said I was a skivvy to the older colleagues. They didn't wanna do it so the only other person available was me. The job required me to put price tags on items of stock using a label gun. It basically shoots a small white plastic tag through a product which then holds the price tag to the selected item. I had to do that on many shoes and pieces of clothing within the shop. The job also required me to stock the shelves.

There were brands such as Fila, Superdry, Adidas and Lyle and Scott. I have never been one for following the latest trends as I have always hated the idea of looking like the man you just passed in the street. I had never got to work on the till as I was fairly new and that needed a certain level of trust to do so. I spent most of the time just filling the empty spots on the shelves with new stock and cleaning the shop floor after the day was over. I honestly couldn't deal with the annoyingly rude shoppers.

I had never been in a workplace before as I had only left school a few months prior to the job. I remember one day I was at work and the job just got to me so much. It wasn't anybody at all, it was just the job itself. I hated being the skivvy, doing the same day in and day out every week. I wanted a new job, a more fulfilling one. I had one day gone on my lunch break. I left the shopping centre Kingsgate for a cigarette and something to eat. I had thrown on my green leather jacket, that jacket was honestly my all-time favourite coat.

I walked on out the Kingsgate entrance and began walking home. That was me done! I had left my job half way through the day and went home to tell my mother. I never returned again, I was so glad I didn't have to go back the next day. I felt a sense of freedom from the ball and chains of the workplace. My second job I had was working at Wynsors World Of Shoes. I had also worked there for a few months until I left abruptly... again. I was a shop assistant who had to stock the shelves with an array of footwear and tend customer's needs.

I had to also vac the shop floor from top to bottom at the end of the day but it wasn't too bad, as there was more space for me to breathe. I wasn't bombarded with clothes hanging over my head as I vacuumed the floor beneath it. It was just a wide open space for me to maneuver Henry the hoover about. I remember this lass that worked there who was around twenty-six years old and to be honest she was quite a beautiful person. I was only sixteen so she was ten years older than me. I was anxious to be around such a lovely woman.

She had once asked me "Hey Brandon you should come to mine one day, we can play on my PS3 and eat pizza." I replied nervously "Yeah that'd be nice that, thank you for the offer." I didn't end up going to her's as I was too much of wuss to follow up the offer. I don't know if it was because I was sixteen and nervously new to the world. I was too shy to go there but honestly looking back now I bloody wish I did. She didn't wanna play on the PS3 and eat pizza. She wanted to sleep with me, I know she did.

I could tell by the way she looked at me with those 'I want you eyes.' She was gorgeous I ain't gonna lie. She had brown hair, sun-kissed skin, hazel coloured eyes and a beauty spot on one of her cheeks below her eye. I did have an attraction to her. I was just too scared to take her offer. I remember always chatting to her when on my shifts at work. I loved it when she was on shift as she always had conversations with me. I did like it there compared to my previous job at BANK Fashion.

It was a more relaxed and enjoyable job. I remember standing about waiting for customers to flood the store but honestly that never happened. There was more of a flood in the staff toilet than on the shop floor. I had worked there for a few months until one day I left unexpectedly. I had just had enough as it was quite draining and to be honest extremely boring! I felt it wasn't going anywhere as I wasn't gaining anything. I left on good terms with my boss and work colleagues but it was time to hang up the oversized, traffic cone orange work shirt.

The third job I had was working in a cafe in Huddersfield town centre. I was around seventeen at this point, I had never worked in a cafe before so I didn't really know what to expect. I started off washing then drying the dishes, coffee cups and cooking utensils as the cafe sold food as well. I had spent hours washing up and cleaning around the cafe. I was the only guy who worked there as the rest of the staff were female.

I felt pretty outnumbered and a bit lonely as the

women who worked there didn't have anything in common with me. I certainly didn't with them. There were around six women. They had all worked there longer than me and had got to know one another already. I was civil and friendly with them all but I wouldn't have spoken to them outside of work. I felt strange working there as what I could honestly talk about to these women? I was a seventeen year old boy and they'd left school a long time ago.

I was fresh out of school and I had no clue about life or the workplace. As my job went on it required me to serve food to customers and make them coffees also. I used to clean around the cafe using a mop and vac. I also wiped around the tables, then cleared them of all used cutlery, bowls and plates. It was a pretty basic job but I kept messing up the orders and giving the wrong food to customers. I do have a dyslexic memory which at the time I had only recently found out.

I struggled to remember certain numbers on the orders and had a difficult time remembering what went where and how it went. It all used to get muddled up in my head, then I would become terribly frustrated with myself and the job. I remember one day I was working on the grill doing paninis and sandwiches. I had got an order mixed up with another one. I was scowled at by customers and made to feel stupid by a work colleague as she said to me "Oh Brandon how bloody hard is it? You have to do it like this!" She said it with a red face and a raised voice.

I just said "Yeah yeah, okay yep." I didn't honestly give a shit after that, I just felt like I was better off working elsewhere. It was funny though because when my work colleague said that to me, my mother, sister and brother-in-law had walked in to see me at work but also to get something to eat and drink. They had heard my work colleague talking to me like shit and my mother had said "Excuse me? That is no way to talk to my son, you shouldn't talk to people like that."

The work colleague of mine had put her head down and apologized as though she was a kid being told off by a headmaster. After that day I had decided to leave the job and look elsewhere. I went into work one final day, picked up my last wage packet, then left the cafe for good. I spent my last wage on cigarettes and an impulsive day out at my local charity shop. I have always cherished the idea of charity shop shopping. I love the fact of being able to buy something vintage or even brand new for a reasonably good price. Well you are giving back to charity and helping a special cause whilst grabbing yourself a bargain.

The fourth job I had was working in a hotel in Leeds, I had got the job offer from Lauren's auntie. I had to clean hotel rooms from top to bottom. Stripping off the sweat, dirt and make-up ridden bedding. I had to also clean the toilets in each room I worked in. I had to wipe all the mirrors down that were full of streaks and splash marks. I had to make the bed in a specific manor, plump the pillows and vac the rooms afterwards.

I remember this one room I had cleaned, I emptied the bin into the cleaning trolley bin. As I did so a used condom fell out and dropped in front of me. Luckily the bloody thing was tied in a knot otherwise it could've been a whole bloody mess. I just shook my head in disgust and carried on my duties, I remember having to clean the public toilets downstairs in the restaurant area. One day I had been cleaning the cubicles and there was shit everywhere. I had so many moments where I just thought 'Forget this job man, I am better than this.'

Another time I was cleaning the loos this one guy had waited until I cleaned the urinals, then pissed everywhere. As though he was saying "Shame on you, you have to clean my piss up." I felt as though I was below everyone I came into contact with, I just felt like I was nothing more than a slave to others. One day I had to vac each stairwell in the hotel, there were like fourteen floors or something. I had to also mop each set of stairs whilst going back down to the kitchen to refill the bucket.

I am surprised I ain't got a hunchback from the amount of times I had to bend down and clean each corner and cranny. I had to also feather dust the window ledges in the hotel lobby, then clean the whole downstairs reception area all on my own. I had never worked in a hotel before so I didn't know exactly how much work had to be done. Another thing that truly got to me was the constant language barrier I had with the other cleaners there. There were Romanian, Polish and Brazilian workers who hardly spoke English.

When I would go on my cig break they would all look at me and talk in their own language about me. I knew this because I would see them smirking whilst looking at me as I stood on my own in the corner. I felt so out of place, like a dislocated bone. It wasn't my place to be there. I was better than that shitting job, no pun intended. I remember working in the laundry room, having to wash all the stinking bedding and towels that had been used for God knows what.

The other cleaners would throw the stained, stinky laundry down the shoot as I waited below in the basement. This one time I remember grabbing some used bedding out of the laundry shoot basket, there was literally some woman's face printed onto the sheets as though she had made a print upon the fabric. There was pink lipstick, fake tan and mascara on the bed sheets. It was in the shape of a face. I mean how can someone wear so much make-up in bed? Maybe she was an escort and had been doing her business with a client.

Lauren used to be an escort before she met me. I know she had mentioned that some nights she would go to different hotels around Leeds. Maybe that same client had used the condom that fell out of the bin as I cleaned that one room. I had moments where I would stay in the kitchen and eat the breakfast items that were leftover from the morning. I remember this one week I was at work, I had gone into the kitchen and ate about two croissants that I had stolen. I was bloody starving as I was living at Lauren's parents' house.

They were so damn stingy with food. I honestly lost so much weight living there, I remember weighing myself and I weighed about eight stone and eight pounds. I was so slim and felt lethargic each day. I mean I wasn't brought up in a rich home or anything but I never starved, ever. Yes they were days that were dire but my mother always fed me, my brother and sister very well. My mother has always, always done her best for us all. She still does to this day, I am truly blessed to have such a wonderful mother.

Anyways, I worked at the Holiday Inn in Leeds for around a month or so until I left. I didn't even get paid at all, honestly. I was told I would be fine working there with just my birth certificate as proof of ID but then once I had left they said "Oh no you needed your passport too, that is why we couldn't pay you." I felt so bloody mugged off, I had basically worked a month for nothing. All those hours I put in each week to just get nothing back, no bloody wonder I was stealing croissants to eat as my breakfast and dinner.

I truly hated that job, I have hated every damn job I have had as I believe I am meant to be someone far greater than those positions I have held previously. I mean it depresses the shit out of me, working in these dead end jobs with not even two pence to hold at the end of the month. I just know that one day I will be exactly where I need to be, having everything that I desire. I refuse to live in such poor ways anymore, always putting in but never getting much back. You ever get the feeling you are meant to be someone great?

I wanna be able to feel the rewards from my hard

work and suffering. I don't wanna be another lost soul, slaving away in some God awful job with a girlfriend who doesn't truly love me, with a family of my own that I never really wanted. That whole aspect of life truly scares the shit out of me. I have seen many poor beings trapped and depressed in their never ending nightmares they call their lives. I remember going to work one day whilst I was at the Holiday Inn in Leeds and I was standing waiting for my bus in Riddlesden to go to Leeds.

I was so damn depressed about the idea of having to go to this job. I had stood in the bus stop shelter downing my Mirtazapine anti-depressants as though they were sweets. I wanted to numb myself whilst I was at work. I honestly hated that job, it was purely soul breaking. One day I had enough and I never returned to that job ever again, I didn't care if it pissed Lauren's auntie off or her mother as I was staying at her's at the time. I was doing it for myself, nobody else.

Chapter 8

I remember when I was in Airedale Hospital in Bradford for four days back in 2017 after I had taken an intended overdose. I took paracetamol, ibuprofen, Tyskie - which is a Polish beer - then a load of other medications I had found in Lauren's parents' medicine cupboard. I had taken about two packets of paracetamol, then a packet of ibuprofen and swallowed it with a four pack of Tyskies. I remember the sickening buttery taste of the dissolving paracetamol as it slowly worked its way down my throat.

I had sat in a nearby graveyard one night on my own whilst Lauren was out in Leeds drinking and being everyone else's girl but mine. I had sat in Riddlesden graveyard looking at the headstones of the dead thinking 'I wonder what kind of person they were and what they did when they were alive.' I have always been intrigued by death and what happens after we die. Not to sound depressing or odd, but death to me means a rebirth of old ways. I believe we go to the spirit world where we meet up with our loved ones and other past folk.

I mean it would be so interesting to speak with my ancestors and loved ones who have been watching me ever since I was born. I would love to meet with them to chat about life and death... to know what comes next once we are in the spirit world. I would love to know who I was in my past lives and where I lived and what my occupations were. I know that death isn't the end, it is just the death of our mortal vehicle which is our body. Our soul lives on for generations and generations at a time, we are far older than our living age, our soul is hundreds of years old.

Getting back to it though, I was sat in the graveyard downing Tyskie after Tyskie. I would swallow tablet after tablet until there were no more left, my stomach burning and aching in agonizing pain, I remember clutching my stomach as though I was about to throw up but I never did. I had been sitting there in the cold dead of night, thinking about my death and what would come next. I had been drinking at a bar down the road for around two hours. I met a couple of guys down there who were also drinking.

One of them had a spliff and I had asked him for a few burns. I had left the pub and wandered up to the local shop to buy myself the paracetamol and ibuprofen. I stumbled into the graveyard then sat down on a bench and began my self-destructive mission. I had never taken an overdose before so I didn't know how long it would take and what would happen to me during one. I know it was selfish of me to do such a dumb thing but honestly I was depressed, lonely and lost to a world of absolute chaos.

I had been sitting in the cemetery for about an hour or two then I made my way back to Lauren's parents'. I remember getting back onto the main road and I saw Lauren pissed up wandering the streets. She had just come back from Leeds, I remember seeing her then saying "Where the hell have you been? I have needed you for the last few hours." She just said "Oh whatever, I have been with my friends." Then she brushed past me and made her way back home. I had walked off away from her, I didn't tell her what I'd done.

I spent another half an hour thinking of my next move, then made my way back to her parent's house. I got back but the house was locked up and all the lights were off. I thought 'Oh for God's sake I am locked out and I can't get a hold of anyone to let me in.' I stood outside for about twenty minutes until Lauren had seen me standing outside the front door. She angrily let me in and said "What the hell do you think you are doing? Get in the bloody house now." I walked on through the front door, then upstairs into Lauren's room.

She was totally pissed and violent. She had slapped

me as hard as she could around my face, proceeding to hit me on my head and punch me in the stomach. I literally stood there taking each kick, punch and slap. I didn't once hit her back. I just burst out crying but still kept the volume down as I didn't wanna wake her parents up and cause a right scene. I told Lauren what I'd done to myself and I said to her "I am sorry for doing it but I am so depressed right now and wanna die."

I remember Lauren had then wrapped her hands around my neck, began strangling me and said to me "You wanna die do you? Okay!" then she proceeded to choke me until I couldn't breathe at all. I had just let her choke me until I burst out in a huge coughing fit. I was so done with her and everything else in my life at the time. I simply allowed her to beat and strangle me. I was used to the beatings and the abuse as she had always done such things ever since we were together. I remember lying on her bedroom floor curled up, crying and experiencing symptoms of an overdose.

I didn't know why she was being so bloody cruel to me, I never hit her once, ever. You never expect the person you love to be so damn evil towards you. I was laid on her bedroom floor awaiting my fate, I remember as I was curled up on the floor she had kicked me in my back, then pulled on my hair. I literally felt so bloody alone, I truly did! I didn't know someone could be so horrible to another person who they claim to love. That wasn't love, it was the definition of hate.

I had finally fallen asleep in a drunken and paracetamol-ridden haze, I awoke with an extremely dull headache and a sharp pain in my stomach. I felt like I was slowly and horribly dying. I got up and dressed. I was wearing a black hoodie, a pair of black trousers and my green Adidas Gazelles. I was still in Lauren's bedroom at this point when I heard from downstairs "Brandon needs to go today, he can't stop here no more." I think it was her mother who'd said that. I couldn't really hear properly but I had proceeded to get my duffle bag packed with all my things.

I then walked down the stairs and out the door with no communication to anyone. I had said one sentence which was "I will go to the job centre or something." I said it as a passing comment to anyone who could hear me. I left the house and headed for Keighley town centre. I walked all down the main road towards Keighley town centre, duffle bag slung over my shoulder with a belly full of Tyskie and paracetamol. I hadn't eaten anything at all that morning or even the night before for that matter.

I was running on toxins only, I remember feeling a sharp pain in my stomach and then a burning sensation that rumbled within me. I felt like I was slowly decaying, rotting away from the inside out. I managed to get to Keighley, I was standing across the road from the job centre. I was outside the Peacocks clothing shop. I was standing there for about ten minutes when I saw this woman who must've worked there. I said to her "Excuse me love, please ring an ambulance, I have taken an overdose."

Something inside of me just went 'Brandon you need to tell that woman now.' I had told the woman and then she rang an ambulance for me. I remember leaning against the wall outside of Peacocks when all of a sudden I collapsed onto the ground. I began to throw up this yellowy black stomach lining, retching but no solids were coming up. Just a load of my stomach lining and some fluid which could've been the Tyskie from the night before. I remember laying on my back with my eyes partially open.

I looked up and there was a circle of people standing over me. I had no clue where these people came from but they were everywhere. I had never had such an experience before. I closed my eyes, lying there in pain.

The ambulance arrived, the paramedics got me into the back of it and began doing checks on me. I remember all of a sudden hearing "Brandon, what is going on?" It was Lauren. She had followed me to Keighley, she said "I thought you'd be here as I heard you say back at mine you were gonna go to the job centre."

I laid in the ambulance with Lauren sitting beside me. I don't know why the hell she was actually there as the night before she was kicking the shit outta me. It was such a strange occurrence as why would she do all that the night before but then on the other hand stay with me in the ambulance. I wasn't in the mood to do anything at all, I just felt so done with everything. I got to Airedale hospital, I remember being booked in by the paramedics in the admittance part of A&E. I was then checked for my blood pressure, heart rate and overall observations.

I was put into a wheelchair as I was so bloody weak and felt I would collapse at any moment. I had a drip put into my arm to flush all the toxins out of my system. I sat in A&E with Lauren beside me, the IV drip had begun taking effect and I started to throw up into one of those grey egg box-style bowls they give you in hospital. I sat there throwing my guts up, all that was coming present was my stomach lining and a horribly phlegm-like fluid which I presume was the alcohol and the array of pills I'd swallowed hours before.

I felt on death's door, I remember sitting there in the waiting room when this woman had come and sat near us in her wheelchair. She was jaundiced and had a massive gash in her head. There was dried blood all down her face and body, her eyes were bloodshot and yellow. It was scary to see such a yellow person, she looked like she belonged in *The Simpsons*. I overheard her saying to her son "I wasn't drunk when I did this, I tripped over the corner of my bed." I had put two and two together and came up with the conclusion that she had been pissed up and tripped over her bed.

She was scarily yellow with jaundice, to be honest she reminded me of what Lauren could look like in a few years time. I had never ever seen a person of such colour before, drinking is such an awful addiction. I sat there for a few hours until it felt dark outside. I was then taken to a ward where I was given a bed and hospital clothing. I had never stayed in a hospital before so I was pretty anxious as to what happens next. I remember being laid across from an old man, he was quite elderly, must have been about eighty-odd.

I remember him saying to me "What are you in here for lad?" I replied "I took an overdose, I tried to end my life." He just looked at me with these sorry looking eyes and then said "Oh no no, you shouldn't be doing that, you're a young man and have all your life ahead of you." I sat there for a moment when the words of his sunk deep within my heart and mind. I stopped what I was doing and I sort of just thought about my life for a moment. I guess he was right, I do have all my life ahead of me.

I suppose in those awfully depressing moments we have, we don't think of the future, only the sorrow filled present. I mean I now feel completely different to back then. I wouldn't ever think of doing such a thing again, I have seen the destructive torment it does to those close to us. It was my first night in hospital and the hours passed by. I had settled into my surroundings a little bit more, then I had wandered outside with my drip in my left hand to smoke a cigarette and to think about my actions.

I remember being stood in those green hospital smoking shelters with a nurse and two other patients. It was pitch black with only the dazzling street lamps overhead, it was becoming winter time so it was bloody freezing as well. I had finished my cigarette and wheeled my drip back inside, then onto the ward where I was staying. I had got into bed as by this point it was pretty late into the night. The next day, I awoke to a nurse changing my IV drip. She was ever so friendly and gentle, I felt compassion in such a huge way compared to how I'd felt recently.

I just felt safe and sound, I didn't tell my mother or anyone else for that matter that I was in hospital. I wasn't on good terms with my mother or my family as I had fallen out with them due to me being with Lauren. I stupidly picked a girl over my family, I burnt my bridges with them all for a long period of time. I do feel so damn badly for choosing an evil bastard over the woman who gave me life. I was far too wrapped up 'in love' and Lauren's twisted ways. I am sorry to my mother and my family for the selfish and horrible things I have said and done.

I was just young, extremely naive and manipulated in so many damn ways. I remember lying there in my hospital bed feeling so lonely, I felt like I was back in that cemetery on that cold night. I couldn't call anyone to make me feel better, I couldn't reach out to have a shoulder to cry on. I was purely alone in all formats. I had my drip changed, then I was given a meal card. It's a card where you tick what you want for your breakfast, lunch and tea. I had not felt up to eating that morning so I just left it unticked.

I then carried myself outside into the cool winter air, I sparked up my cigarette then stared up into the morning sky. I felt like I was in a different world, a much safer one. I was in a blanket of safety and comfort, I didn't wanna leave the hospital as I had nothing out in the real world to hold onto. I had nothing much to do whilst in hospital so I had begun doing random sketches of faces and of things that were in my vicinity. I remember sketching a soldier from World War Two at one point, I had borrowed a WW2 magazine from that old man across from me.

I sat there with crossed legs in my bed with the

wooden table bedside as my desk. I couldn't do much else but relax and feed my mind with positive activities. I have always loved the idea of meeting people from all walks of life, getting to know them as people and what drives them within life. I had met a man called Viktor whilst in hospital, he was on another ward that I had been transferred to on my second day in hospital. Viktor was sitting in the bed opposite me. He had been admitted due to him having an open fracture, caused by him falling off a set of ladders which were clipped by a car that his neighbour was in.

He told me "Yeah I was fixing my neighbour's garage roof and because she was elderly she lost control of the wheel as she was reversing out the garage and clipped my ladders which caused me to land on my wrist and my bone popped out." I replied "Jesus Christ, that is mad, what did you do next?" He had then explained to me "I saw that my bone was popping out and so I tried to push it back in." Urgh... man that is nasty, I honestly don't know how he did such a thing.

I have always hated broken and open fractures. I remember being at school when I was in Year Seven, a few of us from my year were in the tennis courts with the Year Elevens when this kid in my year had decided to grip hold of the tennis court netting, he then ragged on it whilst the Year Elevens were also pissing about with it. I remember he'd been holding one side and the Year Elevens the other side, when all of a sudden I heard this awfully disgusting sound like a bone popping out of place. It just didn't sound real, it was like an extremely distinct sound that echoed through the ears of everyone around.

I remember the kid whose arm was screaming "What's happened to my arm? Why does it look like this?" It looked like a U-bend you find under your sink, his arm was all bent up and broken. I still remember that from about ten years ago, I have felt sick about it ever since. I hate how it looks and sounds when bones break. I mean I have a strong stomach with most things but I can't deal with vomit, snot, broken bones and shit. I don't mind blood or gore to a certain degree but honestly all that other stuff makes me feel ill. I mean blood doesn't smell compared to actual shit or vomit, it ain't too bad.

Anyways I was talking to this man Viktor about his fractured wrist. He had been in hospital for a while as he was fairly old and needed to have more time in due to his age as there could have been a possibility of infection to the open wound. I had already been in two and half days by this point so I was getting used to my surroundings alright. I had my IV drip in for twenty-one hours, then had it taken out as by this point I had flushed all the toxins from my body. I felt much better mentally and physically.

I didn't wanna leave as I had no fixed abode and could not go anywhere in particular as I had burned many bridges with family. I mean don't get me wrong if I told them I was in hospital due to an overdose they would come and see me then definitely let me stay at one of their homes. My family are wonderful and I couldn't ever ask for a better one. My mother is a savior to us all, she is knowledgeable, extremely caring and honest.

I remember being in the TV lounge that patients could chill in, I had met a guy who had pneumonia and was in a wheelchair. He was a friendly guy but had major issues with his mental and physical health. He'd asked me "What are you in here for lad?" I replied "I had taken an overdose mate." He wheeled himself over to me and said "Ah man you shouldn't be doing that bro, it ain't good, you gotta look after yourself." I kept receiving words of advice from many other patients and nurses. They all taught me about taking good care of myself and explained that life is worth living.

I had not exactly been kind to myself nor my body.

I was around a self-destructive and evil girlfriend. She had not exactly been the cleanest of people and she didn't really take care of herself so I guess it rubbed off on me. I suppose what you are around you eventually become. I had gone outside with the guy who was in the wheelchair then he said "You ever smoked a joint?" I replied "Yeah yeah, why?" He then pulled out a little spliff and said "Because I have one now and wanted to know if you want to smoke it with us?"

He was dying slowly and I felt lonely so I excitedly said "Yeah man sure, I could do with a couple of burns." We both went off the grounds of the hospital, we shared this little spliff. I mean the poor man was dying, he had one and half lungs due to one of them being partially removed due to the pneumonia spreading. It probably wasn't a good thing he was smoking a joint but he told me "Listen mate I don't care me, I know I am gonna die soon, I ain't stopping weed it is my only thing I can enjoy so freely."

We had smoked a spliff then headed back to the hospital entrance. I had sparked a cig up when the guy in the wheelchair said to me "I'll catch you inside pal, respect yeah." I felt truly wanted for once in a while, I had met someone decent enough who wanted to chat to me and not do me over. I hadn't smoked weed in a while so by this point I was feeling pretty stoned. I remember walking into the hospital, I could feel my eyes looking bloodshot and glazed over. I was anxious as I didn't want the nurses saying "Brandon, why are you eyes like that?"

I went to have a lovely and warm shower. I sat on one of those disability shower seats soaking up the beautiful water. I felt cozy and so relaxed after that joint, plus with the hot shower. I thought I'd smoke a few burns as I wanted to make myself feel a bit more at ease and at peace with myself. It worked, don't get me wrong, at the end of the day I had tried to do myself in a few days prior so I felt I deserved a little comfort spliff. I remember sitting in the shower for about forty-five minutes just thinking about everything that bobbed into my head.

I felt so safe with no rush to do anything. I had up until the point of being admitted into hospital, lived a hectic life. Oh even after I was discharged I had been released back into a shit storm of drugs, homelessness, alcohol, abuse from Lauren and my own demons that were fighting me day through till the bloody night. I remember eating the hospital food which to be honest was pretty tasty, I loved the chocolate sponge and custard. I also adored the delicious chicken, roast potatoes, mixed veg and gravy meal.

I felt like I had not eaten such a wholesome meal since I was at home with my mother. I especially wasn't eating right living at Lauren's parents' house, I had lost a few stone living there and due to me walking miles nearly every day. I remember walking around the hospital on my own, wearing my mint green Gazelles with my matching hospital gear. I felt like I was in another world, I didn't speak to anyone from the outside, apart from Lauren who came to see me now and then.

I mean even when she did visit me it didn't feel genuine, it was like she was trying to prove a point. Not only a few days prior to my admittance did she mentally and physically abuse me. She was well and truly messing with my mind, I just wasn't smart enough to realise it sooner. I just wanted to go home, back to my mother's in Liversedge. Ever since I left Liversedge I have not felt at home anywhere else, it is like I have been wandering for years. Trying to find my home again, I have felt like I have been living outside of my actual body all this time.

I have lost parts of myself along my journey throughout life, then gained fresh parts of other knowledge in return for my old ways. I had spent a further day in hospital then I knew that it had to happen sometime soon. I just couldn't face the fact of being let out into the world again, not so soon. I had nothing to call my own or my home. I have always wondered what my purpose is and what my main goal is within life, but oh I am still trying to wander the abyss and find the golden piece that completes my life.

I don't even think psychiatric nurses could fathom my mind and tell me what exactly is going on. I have spoken to many nurses, doctors, psychiatrists and people of that profession. Honestly they don't have a clue what is going on with me. I guess it is all down to me, it is down to me to find my true purpose and my soul's mission. I don't believe anyone could tell you what to do with yourself as each and every soul is different and is here on earth for a completely individual reason.

Yes we may have family, friends and partners who relate to ourselves but deep down we are far more apart than what we think. I guess this is why I don't relate to others well at all, I feel like I am a different species compared to the rest of the world. I just feel like I am meant for something much, much more beautiful and golden than the average soul. I ain't saying I am better than anyone else but I just don't fit in anywhere at all.

I have been a skinhead, I have been a punk. I have been a goth, I have been a tracksuit-wearing geezer. I have been a new romantic, I have been a smartly dressed lad. I have been a skater and I have been a vintage dresser. I have dressed in my own ways and means, I have been a chav and I have been a raver. I have dressed in nineties clobber and I have been a rocker. I have been a mod and I have been a streetwear freak. I have been a casually dressed man and I have dyed my hair countless times. I have hung around with all kinds of characters and beings.

I have spoken the different tongues of subcultures

and I have acted in desired ways. Still I just don't cling to no place or person. It is like I am formless, I am just an energy that can morph into any shape. You remember that guy from *Terminator*, the naked guy who turns into a cop and is made from liquid metal and he can transform into anyone he wants. I feel like that, I have been so many different people that I have so much knowledge on everything I talk about. I see people trying to fit in and be like everyone else but honestly I don't wanna fit in like that.

I don't wanna be like everyone else, I just want my own style of life. I bloody hate copycats and followers, it just makes me think you are obviously quite sad, why would you act as somebody else just to fit in and be liked? I couldn't care less if nobody liked me or nobody wanted to hang around with me because I don't dress like them. I wasn't put here to be like you or anybody else for that matter. I was born separately to you and to the rest of the world, if I was meant to be like you I would have been beside you at birth.

We were all born individually to each other, with our own character and details that the universe blessed us with. I am not like anybody else, ever. I am truly something unique and golden, I am a multi-cultured being with knowledge as long as my mental health history. I feel like I am an alien amongst sheep, I am a foreign species to the human one. I may have flesh, blood and bone but that isn't what makes me as a person.

It is my ancient soul that does, I have walked many paths and I have spoken many languages. I have been a whole variety of things, I know my name is Brandon Smith-Johnson but that isn't the whole me. It is just a label to my being, sort of like a product label, it tells you what it is but it doesn't tell you what to do with it. I can be whoever I like and I can be whatever I want, I can shape shift into any space and place. Oh so many past memories gone to the wind, I know many times I have sinned.

Am I losing my sanity or who I am? A war inside the mind of mine worse than the Vietnam War. Countless times my head has banged on the door, intoxicated body lays on the living room floor. Remembering those times I walked on the seashore, oh anxiety ridden movements, lonely and lost, where to now my love? Your looks are pure and resemble up above. Tormented by the abyss, I have screamed many times that life is taking the piss. From town to city through all the nitty gritty, wandering around I hear the snakes begin to hiss.

Backstreets and main roads, seen many different things and many people's modes. Hallways and wards I have yet to receive my rewards, faces of instability I am only wishing for tranquility. Gordon's gin runs every day into a sin, throwing up under the moon behind a corner shop's green bin. Eighteen and naive, oh many nights I have sat and grieved. Thinking of all the times I had believed, double decker bus at seven in winter. Inner city bus ride my feelings I can no longer hide, spotted her in the smoking area I said I would hint at her.

Late night street walking I wandered around in a drunken haze, now I sit and think about all those teenage days. Hoping that one day all the pain will pay.
Reaching out thinking that they will stay, in my bed our warmth can lay. Missing fragments of my mind, I can no longer remember all those times my smile had shined. Leeds streets under the stars, going into different bars and passing all the parked cars. I blinked once and now I am here, oh how time flies just like a spear, I can no longer create a single tear.

Oh those days I could cover a hundred piers, used to rob food to eat, I had to be quick on my feet. Sweating nervously I can hear my own heartbeat, early morning dancing in the street. Living in hostels to hotels to couches and garages, it was a hectic life of course, craving a time to lay in euphoric intercourse. Intoxicated speech I cannot find my way back, kept falling off and on the track. I had nobody to have my back and there were all those times life had a sudden crack.

Tendencies of all kinds used to be completely out my mind, now I journey on to try and find. I must keep a strong spine, eighteen then free, I have been shown all that can be seen. Times were mean and she wasn't so keen, I needed a shoulder so I could lean. Tried to stay awake I needed those coffee beans, on the couch feeling ever so green. I wish you would understand what I mean. Had so many trends yet still no friends, the weight of it all slowly started to bend my life. Pain cut so deep like a kitchen knife, loyalty to one another like husband and wife.

Rose scented candles linger in the bedroom, looking at the stars entwined within the moon. Inside your mind, I would like to end there very soon. Chain smoking thoughts of isolation, I have skipped the trains in other cities stations to see your light. Years going on and on this is a constant fight, crushing blow to my soul it is ever so tight. Those times have gone or are they yet to begin? I am going to be all that I crave and then I shall win. Oh I wanna relive those moments of youth just one more time, before the days of emotional crimes and when life was not fully in the slime.

I will go where the night wind blows and where my light will shine ever so bright. The pain it caused was like a knife to the heart, twisting the blade adding more suffering to the soul. Oh I had laid in the dark hole covered in dirt and tears, so many memories and so many years. I guess that I wasn't just her's as the emotions were a collection of fake furs. Lost to myself, I couldn't have cared about my health and all those times I was left upon the higher shelf. I don't know how to feel love, my heart and soul has been pushed and

159

shoved.

Staying alone for a fear of being loved, my heart was toyed with black leather gloves. No trace of true identity, only feelings of a certain entity, I was left broken and bruised. The pain left my soul feeling empty for my light, I was used and abused. The day of heartache I could have been in newspapers and headline news. Walked miles to see you and by that time I needed new shoes. Had many battles but I still refuse to lose, oh I will never understand why. I am closer to understanding why we all die, how many times did I stupidly believe your lies?

I submitted to the pain as if my hands were in cable ties. Though I knew everything about you just like an informant or a spy, now I live carefully as though my next step I might die. Those tears weren't real, I don't think you can truly cry. I always wonder why though, I can't lie though, life is all planned out similar to a reality TV show. Oh I haven't got the time but soon you will all know, for one day I will finally be the one to glow. I always seem to fall into the traps of the mind and life's enticing alley ways.

Oh I cannot live with anxiety ridden emotions, I feel as though I am far away from this world. Like I am dreaming almost, but in this dream the pain is real and I am awake. Ever since that occurred I have felt so very different, I don't know who I truly am. Only remnants of what was dance within me, all those intoxicant ridden nights. Emerald green gin and sterling cigarettes filled our bodies, wandering loosely at night without a care for anyone but us. Am I that impacted now that I cannot longer live right, oh not living right my darling.

I have felt it more within my dreams at night, I don't know where to go now, I have lost it within my sight. Lonely and irritated I crave to be held within cotton sheets and left to fall into your comfort. I don't know how to live for I have only known how to die, I see angels in the clouds within the sky. I gave away so much but yet I hardly felt it in return, 'Have I lost my care?' I think as the lighter slowly burns. I want to lay beside you and hear all the secrets, taking it in turns. Night time is for when we both deeply learn, "Whatever will happen, will happen" I say to myself.

I'm sick of feeling like I am on the top shelf and I am craving you but you are bad for my health. Isolated days in the flat, I swing around my mind like a baseball bat. Feeling more invisible than a black cat at night, I am hidden in plain sight and the solitary emotions strangle me ever so tightly. I remember the nights on the bus and inside my mind there was no such fuss. The headlights in the distance they burn so very bright. Oh those days are gone and now I see all that was wrong, used to think those times will never fade not like the end of a song.

I feel the marks like a razorblade and I am buried in the abyss. Please pass me the spade, countless times I have lost and not truly gained. Oh how those silly games got played, I am blindly wandering these times and haven't had much rest. The bed is always made and bodies far from laid, oh hazy brain I stare into the mirror and back reflects a bleeding vision. I thought I would know myself by now, I have done much revision. Found the cure but now I must make the first incision. Would you like to come with me?

I only need your decision. I care for the warmth underneath the sheets, the late night dances in the cold dark streets and the caressing of your skin where your eyebrows meet. Oh I know one day I will be in euphoric contentment. You ever feel like you are behind in life, like if you don't do something soon that life will end and you will be a failure? Nobody and nothing could ever teach us the ways of life, for life is a pick'n'mix and each of us shall live differently, love differently and cry differently, oh sometimes I wonder what has the pain been for.

What am I going to acquire for these emotions? Oh I want to be admired, loved and adored. Just like we all must possibly want. I want to be free and content, without the worry of money and isolation. To be free in all possible ways, to do as I please without any sort of stress upon my mind. Life is strange and the events stranger. I feel like I am wandering in the dark night woods, I am craving a sense of light and love. To get me from the shadows and above, bus rides, train rides and so many times I heard all those lies and all I wanted was to run and hide.

Nights I have sat in the cold, chain smoking and solitary I struggled to find the meaning. Art and writing are tools of my tears and all those pain filled years. I feel like I have been at war with myself for too long now, too many injuries of the mind and casualties of the heart. I feel like I have an addictive personality trait and whatever I throw myself into I can't help but be addicted. Oh many times to the wrong things, I am addicted to love in all ways and of one special soul. I just have to capture the light first, I crave a certain satisfaction.

Oh I do not ask for everything just something for me, only things my soul will see. In the sad times we reminisce about the memories we once had and in the chill times we don't think of the past as much. It is so very strange how life works, I always expect something to happen. Like I always expect more from life. I feel like I was put here to get to my golden destination and create a new world, a better world for us all. I do not want to be unheard and poor. Being a nobody who is poor is certainly not a life for anyone.

We all love nice things whatever that may be. I just want to be content in all possible ways, life will happen exactly how it is meant to be. Let us sit back and see what is for you and what is for me. Everything will be euphoric soon, no more need to stress nor worry or be in pain. I will be where I am meant to be in the right time, I will be a winner of life's games. I was taking prescriptions my mind was in submission, gotta work hard for what you want it, is a mission. Spent weeks in the psych wards had many admissions, drinking and sniffing, times of desperate wishing.

I felt for years I had something missing, substance misuse - nah I wasn't the one winning. Waking up and regretting all my past sinning, sat in the doctor's office, was given medication. Pumping pills all throughout the nation, thinking to myself 'Maybe this is the one' like I was looking for a song. Tried and went on like nothing was wrong, the noose I tied around my neck thinking 'How long is this gonna take?' I felt myself dying, I imagined a clear lake, I fell to the floor and said "God's sake."

Chapter 9

I didn't die but now I got too much at stake, never gonna do that again. That was a mistake, so I started sorting through my problems like a gardener with a rake. I wasn't meant to die, I was saved like a slice of delicious cake. Nobody else home but me, unconscious I fell, there was nothing else around that I could see. My neck burns, tears run down my cheek, my stomach hurts but this is one of those lessons I had to learn. Health is precious, once lost it can't be regained. I imagined myself in the coffin, seeing souls of the loved ones I had selfishly pained.

If they found my body I can't be blamed, a mental illness inside I like more than anything to hide. Used to think I was targeted, but on which side? White wine and sterling cigarettes, those are the items of a girl that lied. Wanting to get through to her many times, I had tried but now I love eating healthy, poached eggs and fried. Smoking a roll up I sit on the counter top and drink Kenco coffee granules, I think about the life I now lead. Life is wonderfully, beautifully euphoric, it has its bad days and it has its loveliest of times.

We do not know what will happen next, only if we plan our days we may understand our future but we cannot plan anything in this life my friend. Everything is pre-planned from the universe's perspective, so should we just sit back and relax? Why do we worry about things then? If everything is pre-planned. Our soulmates are already ours but we do not know where they are, that is one of life's beautiful mysteries. It is simply wonderful to know that from birth our life is already pre-made, like a lunchbox from our dearest for the next day.

We know we have work the next day but our lunch has already been made the night before. We plan in advance to make sure we are safe for the next day, but why do we plan ahead when we do not know what will happen next? Our thoughts come from somewhere, somewhere far away from our own realities. We are watched over by the angels and protectors of the spirit world. It is quite lovely to know we are covered for life, better than life insurance from a company with employees that do not know their own life path.

I take a sip of my rocket-fueled brew and think of all the new ways my life could be, living day to day to create a future slowly but surely. Our interests and dislikes all seem pre-planned but how do we know we do not like a certain thing if we have only lived this life once and do not have any memories of living before this life. Like how do our talents and gifts be known when we have not played an instrument or painted before? We surely must have been here for centuries, we have mastered the skills we now use for years and years from the past lives we have lived.

How is it we speak to someone we have never met before or visit a place for the first and yet we resonate with them so much? We must have been here before, we must have. I look upon the sky of stars and clouds and think of life as a learning curve. We are here to learn, learn and learn, experience pain and happiness as one and see what lessons are to be learnt and taken away for the next life. We are one energy living in a shell we call our bodies, we can decompose like flowers and the grass in our gardens but our energies can live on forever.

Our energies are us, our bodies are mortal vehicles that pass through the motorways of life to help us reach our final destination. Picking up passengers of knowledge and passing past places we once visited. Reminding us of what once was, our mortal vehicles run out of fuel so we need to sleep and eat to refuel. We service our machines for further and longer uses, but our soul's energy remains intact for years and years of use. We cannot see our higher selves but we can feel the energy passing through our hearts and minds.

Like a phone charging cable, we cannot see the electric energy charging our phones but we can see the progress of percentage rising and yet we do not question it. Why do we not question our souls, hearts and minds? We question our appearances daily because we can see the effects daily and nightly, but if we saw our internal selves would we treat ourselves differently? What our naked eyes can see we question all of the time but we never truly delve deep into the souls and minds of those around us and ourselves like we do our bodies.

We know what we want to wear or what we want to eat but we do not know what our minds and souls truly desire. We just discard certain feelings and thoughts as if they were a scrap of paper, but yet we do not ask our inner beings what they want, what they need and what they are feeling. Our physical appearance is merely flesh, bone and blood that can be tattooed, pierced, dressed up and transformed. Our minds and souls are not that easily amused with material matters, they crave knowledge, love, power, joy and success in all forms.

They crave truly, deeply, heartfelt emotions and feelings that are more hardened to becoming satisfied. Not through money, not through materialism and not through petty, breakable and burnable things. We are much more than materialism and money, we are the universe, we are limitless. Sometimes I think back to that night when my life was in the balance, I don't think anybody will truly understand me. I felt more alive in moments of near death, let it all slip away until nothing is left, forever alone in this cold world.

Where do I run to? Where is the cure? Maybe there isn't one but death itself. Internal pains destroying my health, marks on my skin from times of crisis. Trying to find a relief from the demons inside, nowhere to run, nowhere to hide. Faking smiles and happiness all those times I lied, God knows I have tried but God knows this

167

shit continues to pry. Can't see a way out, many times the wounds have had to mend. Have you got the happiness I crave that I can lend? Oh alone and suicidal, the razor blades begin to bend.

Praying that this shit will all end, nobody to hold at night when things ain't going right. Too much darkness where is my light? I just want to feel the warmth where things are so very bright. Used to walk around at night, drinking all kinds and high as a kite. Can't see a way out, I am quiet but inside I am shouting, so many times I have tried many damn things. Cold and alone I wait for the angels to sing, waiting for what death may bring. Many years of isolation and pain, I wish I could show you inside this brain and show you the effects; more damaging than a bullet train.

Seeing the blood entwined with water flowing down the drain, from those years ago I am now far from the same. The hurting doesn't stop, no it is far from tame, never was one for fitting in, I was classed as lame. If life was a game, many times I have lost, praying that something new these days will bring. I have not had one, not a single thing. Oh what is all this worth? Suicidal thoughts, thinking of myself within the earth. Tears and blood, is that all I am worth? Days feeling like leaving forever, it wouldn't matter whatever the weather as I have been at the end of my tether.

Oh this broken and bruised soul, lay it in the ground within a deep and dark hole. One thing after another, it is taking its toll, cigarette after cigarette I forever roll. They only think of you when you are either rich or dead, they will never understand what goes on inside my head. If this was America I'd of filled it with lead. Life is beautiful, I simply cannot complain no more as my heart and soul is so full of love and light. I am blessed in all possible ways, I know it has all been part of the universe's great plan, a plan for the utmost success and joy.

All those moments of pain has all been renewed and turned into the most wonderful painting I call my life. Oh I am content and fulfilled, I truly, truly feel blessed. I know that I am on my dream-like journey and all is meant for me and all is happening in the universe's divine timing. I have nothing to fear or worry about, I am protected by the angels and guides of the spirit world, no pain can't and won't last forever. It hasn't in my life, what I desire and crave is already mine, waiting for the next set of keys to unlock all those perfectly crafted doors.

Oh I do not think about the future as it has already happened and is only waiting for me to catch up like copying a simple text from a school whiteboard. What is meant for me and for us all truly won't pass us by. We just have to be patient and calmly wait for the events to sync with our souls and unfold like a newspaper in the lap of a double decker bus passenger on a long journey home. We know we are going to the right destination but we haven't got to press the bell so soon as we will end up at the wrong stop.

We have to enjoy the ride and see the lovely sights on the way, but those aren't our sights to cherish. Our sights are individually created for us, created perfectly in all the right ways so that we can live the true lives we have been blessed with. I know that when things do not go our preferred way, that something much, much more beautiful is arriving shortly. I have gotten this far and still I don't know how I survived the ride but I have and I know that I am guided by the greatest beings who want nothing more than for me to be successful in all my ways.

Enjoy your life, everything happens for a much deeper purpose, we just don't see it in those heated times. Trust in the universe and the universe will tie those loose ends with care and love, stay positive and stay clear minded, everything will always, always work out in our favour, just be patient. Everything that is beautifully made takes its sweet time, carelessness and impatience will lead to sloppy results. Trust the process and let things grow accordingly just like flowers of summer and the moon rising slowly above the clouds in winter.

What will happen, will happen, let yourself be free from thinking too much. I am blessed, we are blessed. I have no bloody clue why my mind tries to kill me, honestly how many cigarettes must I chain-smoke and how many times must I mark my skin and how many damn times must I destroy my house? I truly can't understand why my mind is always trying to do me in, all those words of pain and suffering I desperately scream out. Oh nobody has ever hurt me as much as I have hurt myself, I have cut, burnt and attempted to destroy my body countless bloody times.

I just don't know why my mind does this... am I mentally ill? Or am I gifted and don't know how to handle it? I know my mental health history would say otherwise but I don't want to be another statistic in the records of society. I refuse to be another lost soul gone to suicide, I don't want to be remembered as 'that lad who killed himself.' I cannot make anybody understand what awfully horrible pain I have endured, nobody will truly know will they? I have sat and chain-smoked myself to near death and I have used substances as a form of medication.

I have pained my lovely mother so many damn times and I never bloody meant to. I just don't know what will solve this decaying mind, I cannot help the way I feel from time to time. I had nobody to hold me in those depressingly sad times, I pray to the universe for something more but oh I am losing my faith. I have cried out in despair but nothing reaches out as I pull out my hair. Is this revenge from up above for an evil past life? Why must I slowly kill myself out of pure darkness?

All my damn life I have never been taken seriously at all, always been made to feel like a fool and someone who is just a joke in the eyes of society. God what must I do to make them understand that I am not playing games, I haven't seen any players nor have I seen the score. This must be real life then, this is far from a game as the pain is far too real. Girls and friends are far from in my sight, I have always had the cold shoulder from the opposite sex, am I too weird? Am I too damaged?

Am I lost completely? I truly do not know anymore, I sit and write this with an angered mind and a lonely heart. I have only had one girlfriend before, she cheated on me... several times or more. The one time I know of, I had caught her but oh the other times I was not there. What an unlucky roll of the dice, the first girl I gave my everything to had shattered and torn my life apart. I am over the pain of that now but oh the trust for others is far from solid. I would like to believe all of the suffering I have collected is worth more than gold but oh I beg to differ.

I cannot get close for my fear of heartbroken nights still burns within me. I am sorry to my mother and family most of all as they have done nothing to deserve my destruction and torment, I have nobody else but them and without them I would be dead now. I know it, I would've given up long time ago. I just can't help my mind sometimes, or my heart for that matter. It is like there is a broken switch within my soul. Every now and then it sticks to one side and to get it to transition to the good side it takes all my energy, time and health.

It is like a big, red switch within the fuse box of my soul, it controls everything I am and everything I do. When it is broken that is when everything fails and turns to ash. I would like to try and make you understand what exactly goes on inside this body but

171

oh I do not understand it myself. I still to this day do not know why I am like this, I do not know what causes this inner torment. People only see the destruction after the pain, they never see the inner demons creating the pain.

Only the aftermath of what I have done is seen in reflection to the hurting. It is like there is a demon fighting my inner self and this battle is ongoing. My inner self ties up the demon to prevent any more suffering but oh the demon manages to slip away and take the lid off of things which then causes my life to boil over and burn the foundations I have carefully built. I have been trying to define my pain but oh honestly it's like it is in some foreign language and I do not speak the words it creates.

I have tried medication after medication and I have tried drug after drug but still nothing eradicates the darkness. I have drank liters of alcohol and I have smoked spliff after spliff but oh that too doesn't stop the torture. I have spoken to a variety of nurses, doctors and psychiatrists but they do not have the answers. I have tried and tested many damn things and yet I still have no clue as to what will bloody solve it. Is this me forever? Is this the new Brandon Smith-Johnson?

I look in the mirror and I do not recognize the fragile and lost being that stares back. I see remnants within my eyes of somebody I once knew but now I am not the same person I once loved. I feel lost within my own deep, dark and tormented woods, inside me there is a candle and the flame is nearing the wick. One small gust of breath it shall leave me in pure darkness, I am clinging onto life with sweating palms and oh I am slowly slipping. Maybe there could be a grasp of a savior before I fall into the abyss, I do not want to fall, for the abyss has promised to keep me locked away.

There is a light but oh it is close to going out, it has

been used far too many times and the fuse is close to blowing. It must stay on for if not I not will be seen again, I do not want to live in darkness for the rest of my days. I want to feel the beautifully euphoric love that an angel can gift me as we lay amongst comfort. I want to wake up and feel like I am loved by many and that I am worth more than diamonds. I want to dance in the night and feel free from the shackles of torment. I want to laugh with uncontrollable emotion and I want to lay in silence feeling nothing but pure light and harmony.

I want to look in the mirror and adore the vision I gaze at. I want to be remembered as the one who conquered the demonic suffering and made it big through all the pain. I want to admire and appreciate my every molecule. I want to show the whole world that I am a star and that my light shall never die. I want to take pictures with my fans and I want to inspire millions. I want to help and encourage those who have felt the harshness of life's darkness. I want to be known worldwide for my efforts, blood, sweat, tears and sleepless nights.

I want to feel the rewards from all this brutal torture. I wasn't put here to just roll over and die, I was put here to be a light in the dark and to show the world my souls gift. I am gonna be known all across the globe for turning my sorrow into success. I remember when I lived in Liversedge with my mother. One day I had been watching Spike Island in my bedroom when I had the sudden urge to trek to Cleckheaton for some ice cream.

It was summertime 2017 so the weather was absolutely delicious. I remember wearing a baggy, sunflower yellow t-shirt and my Levi's. I had my sky blue converse shoes to complete the fit. I set off on the half an hour stroll to bag myself some chocolate ice cream, the one in the plastic tubs you can purchase in the freezer aisle of your favourite supermarket. My nearest supermarket was Fulton's Foods, I had left the flat and began walking down the huge hill from High Town down to Cleckheaton.

I cut down a dirt path to pass through the fields and mud-ridden trails. It was summer after all so the mud was rock hard. I didn't get covered in sludge like I did back in wintertime. I remember passing down a street that had a cul-de-sac left right and center. I was walking down on the right hand side of the road when I clocked this elderly woman walking up on the left side. It was extremely damn strange that it was a sizzling hot summer day, yet nobody else was around but me and this elderly woman.

I guess it was meant for me and her to cross paths with nobody else involved. I believe in the universe's divine timing, the universe is the master of all things. It had purposefully set this interaction up for me. I had noticed from the top of the road that this elderly woman was holding her head and carrying what looked to be like a hammer. I thought 'Hang on a sec, what is she doing? Is she alright? She is bleeding like a fountain.' As we both got closer to each other I had crossed the street to her side.

In a raised and concerned voice I shouted to her "Bloody hell love, are you alright? What has happened to you?" She had blood pouring from her forehead all down her jacket and clothing. She was holding her head to try stem the bleeding. In her left hand she was holding a blood-spattered claw hammer. I was so damn gobsmacked with empathy. I had got closer to her then she said to me "I have just been mugged on the Greenway in Cleckheaton, the guy who did it dropped his hammer as he ripped my purse from me."

I immediately replied "Bloody hell, you need to sit down love, have you got anything to stop the bleeding?" I had got her to sit down on this patch of grass beside the roadside. She had a Greggs pasty packet in her handbag.

I rapidly grabbed the pasty packet then asked her to hold it over her forehead. I thought 'Oh man, there is blood pissing out of her head.' My sky blue Converse shoes were now tie dyed with splashes of crimson coloured blood.

Her forehead was slightly dented in, as though the hammer she was carrying had cracked open an Easter egg. She kept saying to me "I am fine, I will go home, I will just sleep it off." Obviously she was in pure shock and riddled with adrenaline. I had never been in such an awfully important situation before. Her life depended on me as if I let her go she could have bled to death and died in her home. Like I said there were nobody else around but me and her, on a bloody summer day as well.

I had been sat with her for around ten minutes but it felt like ten hours. This workman in his van had pulled round the corner then down the street, I flagged him down and shouted "Oi mate come here quick, I need your help." I was waving my left hand rapidly in an attempt to catch his attention. I felt as though I was trying to waft some weed smoke out my bedroom window before my mother caught me with the way my arm was moving. It had worked, he saw me and the elderly woman in a flash.

He jumped out his van then in a highly panicking manner he said "Jesus Christ, what the hell has happened? I will ring the ambulance now mate." While he was on the phone to paramedics I further assisted the woman. The Greggs packet she used as a tourniquet was now red, white and blue. Not how the normal Greggs packets look like. I had never seen so much blood before, she would've defo died if I let her go home. I wasn't allowing that to weigh heavy on my conscience like an overweight person on a see-saw.

The ambulance had arrived in a heartbeat, then they jumped out and began doing their job. I was now splattered with speckles of crimson all down my sunflower yellow top, Levis and sky blue converse shoes. The police had then arrived on the scene. They had begun questioning me, getting the low down on the situation. I had told them everything I knew and everything which I had done. They then took my address, phone number and name so that they could further probe me with questions.

I had then overheard the paramedics saying to one another "Yeah, she possibly has a skull fracture, she is going to need serious treatment otherwise it could be fatal to her life." I thought 'Bloody hell, imagine if she went home and I had just ignored her, she would be dead.' I then asked the paramedics "Have you got anything to clean myself with?" They then handed me a couple of anti-bacterial wipes to rid myself of that poor elderly woman's blood. I was told by the coppers "We will be in touch Brandon, thank you for your time."

I was finally allowed to leave the scene. I then strolled on down to Fulton Foods and as I was patrolling the aisles, looking for my chocolate ice cream my mother had given me a ring. I answered the phone as I was scanning the ice cream selection. I instantly told my mother "You never guess what has just happened to me?" She replied "What, what's happened?" I then began to explain the eventful occurrences that were just in my grasp.

I remember my mother's Yorkshire slang in which she said "Oh wow, bloody hell, is she okay now?" I replied "No pun intended ay mum? Yeah she should be in hospital now, she went a good half an hour ago, I will tell you more when I get back home." The phone call ended then I had rewardingly found my favourite chocolate ice cream. It was like a beautiful gift from the universe as a 'well done Brandon, you done good lad!' I then left Fulton's with a proud grin on my face back to my mother's flat, holding my tub of chocolate ice cream. I was truly proud of my efforts.

I remember when I was on the moors with a few

people from my extremely strange past. I can't remember exactly what the name of the moor was. All I know is that it was the one where you pull into the left off that long road that goes towards Manchester way. It was the one with the reservoir, I can't bloody remember it. Anyways I went up there back in 2019 with a group of people who certainly didn't know what they were doing. Very naive if you ask me, they were young just like me but I for one know much about a lot.

I may be young but that doesn't mean I am stupid. I have had my stupid moments but that was all because I was under the influences of many things. I am extremely mature for my age, I have had to be otherwise I wouldn't have made it out alive at points. I don't compare myself to nobody else but Brandon Smith-Johnson. I am him and he is I... back to it though, I was on this moor with these people and we had all decided to take LSD. I mean it wasn't the brightest of ideas but like I said I was young and under the influence back then.

We had all started to walk around the huge landscape of the moors. It was so beautiful to experience the full-frontal effects of the nature around me. The sun was beaming down on my face whilst the birds sang overhead. I felt totally at peace, like I had no true worries. I remember walking along the side of the reservoir, then looking at the waves of water caressing one another. The LSD had made the water look as though it was electrified and that if one was to touch it, you could be killed within an instant.

I took a photo of the water but my phone was acting strange. Apparently LSD interacts with electronics and can cause them to appear to not work or to work inefficiently. My phone was working perfectly fine on the bus ride up to the moors but once I got off the bus and onto the land of the moors, it began acting strange. We had all gone up there to look for mushrooms but honestly I didn't... I went up there to enjoy the scenery. I love nature, I love how the universe has created and crafted each and every beautifully euphoric detail on this earth.

I love landscapes of all kinds, but the people I was up there with wanted to get as intoxicated as possible. They were very silly as they thought it was a joke to get as messed up as possible on the moors. The moors where people have died due to carelessness. That day could have been a whole lot different, I am just glad I know about these things as I have been up there before. I knew that we had to get off the moors before night-time as it gets Antarctic-level cold up there.

My uncle once told me "There was this lad once who went up to the moors on his own, his phone died when he was deep within the moors. He got lost and couldn't find a way off so he attempted to sleep up there. The next morning some hikers found him curled up in a ball, frozen with both rigor mortis and minus degree temperature." Now my uncle had told me this before I went up there as this was a few months prior to me going up to the moors. I had actually told these people I was with that exact story but they sort of looked at me like I was stupidly making it up.

I said it to them because I didn't wanna be the next guy to be curled up. We all went for a stroll around the grassy hills and over a footbridge to explore the vast landscape. It was pure love up there, I felt peaceful as there were no cars, pollution, people, noise and sirens. It was just the sound of the wind, water and laughter from us all. I have always loved the desolate surroundings within life, I don't like too much noise or chatter. I love to be able to listen to my own thoughts, soul and heart, so I can further increase my wisdom.

We were all up the moors for a few hours until it fell to night-time. It had got deathly cold, people's teeth were chattering... not purposely either. I remember people switching from shorts to joggers and from t-shirts to jackets. I had explained to them "I told you all that I was right, we should've got off the moors before it fell to night." It was scarily windy as well, which made the temperature ten times worse. We had all gone down a dirt path that was only manageable if we all went in single file as there were about a twenty foot drop on the left side of us.

If one of us had fallen, especially at night, we wouldn't have been found till the next day. I remember screaming to everyone "Stay in bloody single file, do you want to die tonight?" I wasn't having some poor sods death on my head, I was like a tour guide to them all. I had made sure everyone stayed together and was safe. We had carried on walking further and deeper into the ghostly quiet moors. We kept going down and down and down until we got to a small waterway.

All of us had stopped at this bit of water and decided not to cross as it was a dead end. If we had of crossed this waterway we would have been meeting our makers soon enough. The water dropped down at least three times so if we crossed over it we would have been swept down each drop. A few people began crying and screaming with absolute fear as they felt this was the end for them. I wasn't scared at all to be honest, I knew we could have got off there as soon as possible but we had to stop bitching and focus.

One of the people we were with had stupidly decided to ring the police and mountain rescue. I felt this was a bloody silly thing to do as I was one of the oldest ones there, plus we were all on LSD and some of the people also had weed on them. So in the eyes of the law I would've been screwed as the police would have seen it as "Well Brandon, you are one of the oldest so you should have known better and you should have not allowed this to happen, also you are all under the influence of substances and are in possession of them."

I didn't want to be caught by the police on the moors

and I certainly didn't want mountain rescue to be aware of this situation either. There were around eight of us, I had decided to retrace my steps back up to the roadside. Me and three other people out of the eight had decided to go back ourselves and try make it off the moors without the mountain rescue or the police knowing. The rest of the people had stayed, I had told them all "Look if you stay here then you will either freeze or you will be picked up by a rescue team and all your parents will know about this."

I didn't wanna be wrapped up in that shite so I asked everyone "Right everyone, you either follow me back and we all make it off here alive or you stay and bitch about it then possibly cause more harm to yourselves." Only three people out of the eight had taken my advice and the four of us had begun walking back up the paths and trails we walked down not only an hour prior. The four of us had made our way back up to the main road where the bus had dropped us off. We waited for the rest of them to appear by the roadside like a set of lost deer.

The three people I was with had said "See, we didn't need no damn helicopter to search for us and we didn't need the police to save us either." We had waited there for around twenty-five minutes for the other set of people, I remember there being this Honda civic driving up and down the road beside us. It was like the driver was looking for prey that night. The driver had clocked the four of us stood at the roadside. I remember him pulling up, it was a Middle Eastern-looking man, with dark, evil-looking eyes.

He had balding hair and a huge moustache, with a demonic grin on his face he said to us "Oh where are all lot you going tonight? Do you want a lift with me?" I knew straight away that this guy was evil, what the hell was he doing on his own driving back and forth up and down the moors at that time at night. I knew that if any of us got in that car we would not have made it home that night, probably ended up buried on the moors somewhere. Forget that, I never accept rides off of anyone besides family.

I have seen too many serial killer documentaries to know that you should never accept lifts off of anyone you don't know. Anyways about ten minutes had passed since the evil man had spoken to us. We finally saw the rest of the group appear. In the distance though I could see that mountain rescue were out looking for us all. There was a rescue helicopter with its searchlight on, scanning the moors for a set of idiotic youngsters. I wasn't one of the idiotic ones mind, I just happen to be with a set of them.

I knew we could get off the moors safe and sound but those other people didn't listen to me earlier that day when I said "We need to make sure we are off by night-time, otherwise there could be trouble." As we were waiting for the next move, a police car had appeared, then pulled into the parking park beside the road. They had said to us all "What the hell are you all doing on the moors at this time? Where do you all live?" We had explained the situation in hand then they offered to take a few of us home as there were only two police cars and eight of us.

The other people I was with had either got a lift off their parents or with their friend's parents back to Huddersfield. I had got a lift off the police with one of the people from the group. Me and this other person I was with had got back to Huddersfield, then walked into the town centre. We had both stopped to sit down on a bench on the piazza to roll a spliff. We sat there, smoked it and spoke about what the hell just happened. I was still living in Edgerton hotel at the time, the hotel where that junkie tried to stab me with the needle.

I had no worries as my parents didn't need to know what happened that night, I was safe from a bollocking. We had finished our spliff and then went our separate ways. I got back to the hotel and had a long, hot shower, I then climbed into bed and shut my eyes. The day was over and so was my trip. I remember when I stayed in a B&B in Wibsey, Bradford. That place was seriously an eye opener to all things wild. I had been staying there for a few months, I think it was around three months or so. I had been staying there as I had been kicked out of the Bradford Foyer for not paying my service charge.

I mean I was glad I didn't pay it as I said earlier in this book 'mice were eating my clothes and people were eating my food.' I couldn't deal with that all the damn time so I guess it was my opportunity out of that place. In this bed and breakfast there were people of all backgrounds and walks of life. I had been moved around the B&B about three times, the reason being is that because I was a longer-staying guest and the rooms I had been staying in were meant for families so they'd move me to a smaller room.

I was grateful for the roof over my head and the free breakfast in the mornings but honestly the guests were unsavory. I had met this one guy who had one leg missing due to him hitting a piece of his flesh with a heroin-riddled needle. Instead of injecting into his vein he missed and then his leg was filled with heroin. He was hobbling around using crutches but honestly he was not exactly the nicest man. He was a big dealer of drama, he liked to cause arguments and see them unfold whilst laughing his head off.

He would sit and say something to another guest to get a reaction from them, then act like they are the ones who are argumentative. I remember one night I was staying in a room at the bottom of some stairs when I had heard some commotion going on at the top of the stairs. I had wandered out of my room and peeked my head up the stairwell when I noticed the guy with the missing leg and some other guy who had a serious drinking problem were being loud and disturbing. I had asked "What's going on mate? Everything alright?"

At this point I had already got to know these two men a little bit as I had been staying in the bed and breakfast for a couple of weeks. The guy who had one leg replied to me and said "Yeah everything is fine but he is out of his head on something." He was referring to the big drinker who was stood at the top of the stairs not moving a muscle, just staring into the wall in front of him. I thought 'This is extremely worrying' as he literally looked like he was out of his body and his body was just vacant and dead.

He was stood staring into thin air with his eyes bulging outwards and scarily wide open. It looked as though he had taken three bags of coke, proper wide-eyed and bloodshot. I asked the guy with one leg "Why is he like that? What has he taken?" He then replied "I gave him some e's." I was just like "Oh bloody hell, he is proper out of it isn't he." The big drinker was still in a comatose state and still he didn't mumble a single word. I knew that he wasn't on ecstasy as he wasn't bouncing around the hallways as you would be if you did take some pills.

He was defo on something much more sedative, I had been stood in the stairwell for a good ten minutes or so when the guy with one leg had given the big drinker a devastating punch to the face. His nose began to piss out blood all over the place, his lip was also bust open. He had blood all down him but he still didn't make a sound or move a muscle. He was surely on something much worse than ecstasy, I had later found out that he was on heroin... the guy with one leg had given it to him.

The big drinker was really damn out of it, like scarily vacant from his mortal vehicle. I had then gone back into my room and began watching television. I remember stood there thinking 'What the hell am I doing in this place? When am I getting out of this negative-infused bed and breakfast?' There was this other time I was in the hallway of the bed and breakfast, I had been wandering around trying to find a lighter off one of the other guests when I had stumbled upon an open door.

The door lead into a Scottish man's room. I was stood outside his room, then popped my head into his doorway. I could see that he had no legs and he was screaming whilst rolling around on his bed. He was in some proper messed up state of consciousness from heroin, it was so damn scary as he was making some awfully strange sounds. He didn't say any words or anything, he was just making saddening cries. The Scottish man was rolling back and forth on his bed, his screams were getting louder and louder as he ventured deeper into his heroin-induced state.

He was so very fragile looking, as though the wind could have snapped his spine if he was to be caught in a storm. I remember this young lad walking past me and saying "What the hell is that noise?" I replied "This man is overdosing or something, he is proper in trouble." The young lad had then leaned into the Scottish man's room and said to me "Oh nah he isn't overdosing, he is just on heroin, I know who he is." I had then asked the young lad if he had a lighter I could use, he said to me "Yeah man I'm going outside now for a cig, come out with me."

I went outside with the young lad and sparked my cigarette. I couldn't believe that I was around these sorts of damaged beings, I am not judging them at all but honestly I hated being around that environment. Heroin, alcohol and substances lingered in nearly every room and in the bodies of those inside the rooms. It felt like I was there for three years not three months. I would always leave the bed and breakfast every day as I couldn't stand the constant arguments, cries and crack smoke that danced through the hallways.

Chapter 10

I was in a skid row-type B&B where anything and everyone went. I was never around such substances like heroin and crack until my feet landed in that main entrance. I had seen that sort of shit only in films like *Trainspotting* but never in person did I experience such moments. I remember this other time I was in there and the guy with one leg had been smoking crack in his room as I could always smell the stale remnants of it dancing around the hallways. The B&B manager didn't ever say a word to them.

He spent most of his time next door in his beautifully manufactured home, away from all the drama and disease. He was surely making a lot of money from these souls as the council in Bradford had put them in there for a short while until they had somewhere else of their own. I had also been dropped in the B&B from the council as like I said earlier, I had no place to go besides there as I had been kicked out of Bradford Foyer. I mean it could have been a whole lot worse, but it also could have been a whole lot better too.

My first night in that B&B were pretty wild as I remember being in a dingy, smelly and cig-burnt room. The shower was rusted and spattered with dirt and grime. It was cold as the windows were quite old and hadn't had been double glazed and the radiators were broken and vintage-looking. I remember I laid in my bed with tears in my eyes thinking 'Where the hell am I? This ain't my home, I don't need this shit.' I had then tried ringing Lauren but she didn't answer me, she had later text me saying 'What do you want? I am with my friends.'

I had just come out of Airedale Hospital at this point, the hospital I was in due to me taking that overdose in Riddlesden graveyard. I had been dropped into that bed and breakfast for a few months until like I said somewhere better came along... it never did. I was in there for months on end, I remember that first night I was in there, I had tried ringing Lauren again but no answer came from her. I knew that she was at her friend's flat in Keighley so I had decided to run from Wibsey all the way down to Bradford Foster Square station in the city centre.

It took me forever to get there but I successfully managed to make my way there. I got to the station and I spent my last few quid on a single train ticket to Keighley. I had been in such a depressingly sad mindset, I just wanted my 'girlfriend' to hold me and tell me "Everything is going to be fine babe, don't worry!" How bloody wrong was I, she never said that to me ever! I got to Keighley, then made my way to her friend's flat, but they weren't in... I remember screaming in the street "Bloody hell man, damn, damn, damn!"

I had like five percent on my phone and Lauren still wasn't answering her phone. She was just ignoring me, she didn't answer one bloody phone call, I felt the same level of loneliness I experienced back in that steel cold graveyard in Riddlesden. The same night I had taken that overdose, I was so damn sad, man. I couldn't ring anybody, I was still not on good terms with my family so that was a big no. I had no friends so that was also a massive no and the only person I had in my life was a violently awful alcoholic 'girlfriend.'

I had no chance at compassion in that period of my life, I was far, far away from home, never mind sanity. I felt my world slipping into the abyss. I was so bloody lost and so very damn tired of everything. I hadn't been out of Airedale for more than a week and my life was back into the bloody drain. I had ran into the Weatherspoon's in Keighley, I had sat down by the window side and began charging my phone. I was in there around an hour or so but with each minute that went by I was desperately peering out the window to see if I could spot Lauren and her friend.

The streets were eerily quiet with not one soul in sight. I honestly felt so screwed as I didn't have any money to get back to the darkened bed and breakfast nor did I have much time left as Weatherspoon's was shutting soon. My phone didn't have full battery either, my hands were tied so what could I do? I had decided to go to Lauren's friends' flat and ring her buzzer to see if they were back. I got to the flat and I remember looking up at the windows and I could see that there were lights on in the front room.

I immediately rang the buzzer in despair, Lauren's friend had answered the buzzer with an intoxicated and slurred voice. She had said "Hello? Who is this?" I then replied "It's Brandon, please can you let me in? I need to see Lauren." She was proper out of it, she was on drugs or something. I remember Lauren coming to the buzzer and saying to me "What are you doing here? Why are you here Brandon?" I then replied back "I need to see you, I am sad, I need to speak with you." Lauren said "God's sake Brandon, right, one minute."

She came down the stairs and into the street to speak with me. I told her that I was sad and needed my girlfriend, I didn't want anybody else but her at that moment. She wandered towards me and looked at me, her eyes were mangled with intoxicants. One eye was looking past my right shoulder and the other eye was looking past my left. I said to her "What are you on? Why are you wasted? Why do you have to do drugs Lauren?" She then replied "Oh shut up Brandon, how can you talk? I am doing what I want."

I just started to cry because I was so very hurt that she would ignore me for so many hours just so she could get messed up on drugs and drink. I felt so alone... I had told her "Please come with me back to the B&B, I don't want you to be doing this to yourself. Why can't we just be together tonight without any drugs or wine?" We had been stood outside for a good twenty minutes or so when she started to get angrily violent towards me. She always started to become violent with me every time she past her limit, she had started to slap me because I told her some home truths about her drug and alcohol intake.

She had picked up a metal pole she found down by a public bin, then began hitting me with it on my legs and my arms. I had said to her "If you carry on I will ring the police Lauren, I can't deal with you being violent all the bloody time, stop damn hitting me!" She was slurring her words, stumbling the streets and still hitting me. I would've been best to not have come that night, I should've stayed at the B&B. Time past and we weren't moving from the streets and she wanted to go back into her friend's flat.

After a good half an hour or so she ran back into the flat and left me outside. I began to scream in inner pain, crying as I sat on the curb outside. Nobody to hold me nor tell me things will be fine, I just sat there smoking endless cigarettes wishing this pain would end. I remember these three guys coming out of Lauren's friends' flat, one was her friend's boyfriend and the other two were his friends. They had said to me "You better piss off away from here, go away now!" I replied "Nah I ain't going anywhere until Lauren comes back out."

They then said "She doesn't wanna see you so go away, you aren't welcome here." The three of them were also wasted on drugs and drink, acting like the proper low-life scum they were. I remained on the street, I wasn't scared of three dossers like them. I have been around evil people and these three were mice compared to them. I had said "Oh three against one is it? You lot are hard aren't ya?" They stood in a line beside one another not getting anywhere with me, I was just laughing at them as I truly didn't care no more.

I was just in a whatever-goes mindset. I wanted to

stitch them all up because I knew I could take on three of them at a time, plus I wanted to get back at Lauren and her idiotic friend so what I did was, I rang the police. The three of them had darted back into the flat as soon as I said "Watch now then, the police are coming you little bastards." They scarpered and locked the door. I had told the police "Hi yeah, there is a group of people trying to fight me and they are all taking drugs in public, I am fearing my life."

I wasn't fearing my life but I knew with some added emotion the police would be there in seconds... they arrived straight away didn't they. The police came and entered the flat, I don't know what they were told or what they did inside but I know they all shat themselves as soon as the blue lights came flashing round the corner. I looked up at the living room window and I could see Lauren looking at me from above. She was shaking her head at me and sticking her middle finger up, I had then waved at her and smiled.

I was done with her and life that night. The police had come back outside the flat and began to chat to me. The police said "Where do you live Brandon? We can take you back there now." I replied "I am staying in a B&B in Wibsey, I have just come out of hospital due to me taking an overdose. I wanted to see my girlfriend but when I came down here tonight, she was wasted on drugs and drunk, then began being violent towards me." They then replied "Right, okay Brandon, do you want to speak with a mental health nurse now and see if you can get a visit from them tonight?"

I just said "Yeah please, I feel so alone so maybe it would do me good." I climbed into the back of the police van then one of the officers had handed me their phone to speak with a mental health nurse. I sat on the phone for a good twenty minutes speaking with a mental health nurse about the nights events, nothing happened further on their part so I was then taken back to the bed and breakfast. The police had dropped me off outside the B&B, then said "Take care Brandon, get some sleep mate, you wanna stay away from your girlfriend if she is being like that with you. See you later lad, have a good night."

I walked miserably into my cold dark room, I laid on my bed and burst into tears. I felt so bloody let down, I felt like I was in some isolated nightmare but the pain was truly real. There was no waking up away from the torment, I was wide awake and in full pain. I sparked a fag up as my tears slid down my cheeks. I laid there freezing, solitary and sad, what could I do? I was on my own... just like how it always had been back then. I remember when I lived in this hostel in Fartown, Huddersfield, I had lived there for around two months until I moved into my actual home in Holmfirth.

The same house where I would find out the heartbreaking news that Lauren had cheated on me with my awfully evil neighbour. The hostel in Fartown was above a corner shop, so it wasn't bad for the purposes of shopping and cigarettes. Inside the hostel there were four other rooms that housed other tenants like myself... well not like myself in the matter of lifestyle and looks. I remember there being this one lad also called Brandon which I found so very strange as we were two completely different people.

The only thing that tied me and the other Brandon together at the time was that we both smoked weed... I don't know if he still smokes weed now but I definitely don't anymore. He was a sound lad who was easy to chat to, he wasn't evil in any way, not like the other hostel goers I had met prior to this hostel. He was a down-to-earth guy, we used to chill most days as we both didn't have jobs at the time so we used to sit and smoke together. I remember that he was once telling me how his girlfriend had cheated on him, then left him for somebody else.

How bloody strange is that? He had been cheated on

by his girl, then three months later I was cheated on by my girlfriend. I find it so weird how we are both called Brandon and our girlfriends had cheated on us both. Life is surely a beautifully strange thing. When he told me his girl had cheated on him, I said to him "Oh bloody hell man, that is shit isn't it, I am sorry for that mate!" At that moment in time I had never been cheated on... well not that I know of anyway. I had always heard of saddening stories of people being soullessly cheated on by their so called lovers but it had never happened to me like it had those poor beings.

I have never, ever cheated on anyone I have spoken to, never did I cheat on Lauren. I couldn't ever bring myself to do such a heartless crime. I remember this other guy who lived in the hostel, he too was a sound guy, but this one time I remember me and him staying up till six in the morning drinking E&J brandy whilst doing lines of cocaine. I was in a very self-destructive mindset so of course I was gonna do the lines and drink the neat brandy. Me and this guy had been sat in his room just talking about life and what we wanted from its juicy gifts.

We had spoken about our past and what we were doing in this hostel. I remember talking for hours about women, money, mental health and how life is damn weird. I remember the guy always asking me "Ere' mate do you fancy going round to the shop for me and getting some more E&J?" We had drank about four bottles of the stuff, I was at the point of passing out but I kept getting an instant rocket fuel which hit my mind as he had also bought three bags of cocaine in separate intervals.

I know it was mindlessly stupid to have drank and sniffed so much but honestly those days are well and truly behind me now. I don't like to regret as I take all of my regrets and turn them into lessons for the future. I do not look behind me as I feel there is nothing to gain in the past. I only look at the present time and bathe in the qualities of the now rather than what has been. Anyways, I remember me and this guy staying up late just having a laugh and talking about everything and anything.

I felt like I was finally in a hostel that wasn't trying to do me over or do my head in. Yes I know I was around negative influences but at least I wasn't paranoid of getting robbed or attacked as I slept in my room. I remember me and this guy leaning out of his window, talking to these prostitutes. Don't worry I didn't want any business, I was just coked up and extremely pissed out of my mind. We were just harmlessly chatting to passersby and whoever was around at the time.

I remember we were talking to this one lass who sadly was a girl of the night. She was such a nice girl, you could sense that, but she unfortunately had many layers of sadness behind her sky blue eyes. She must have been quite young, maybe early-twenties or so but the drugs made her look as if she was in her late-forties. I remember her asking the guy who I was with "Ay you are not bad looking you, do you want anything?" I just stood there in his room with a heavy look of confusion plastered upon my face.

I honestly feel so truly sorry for these women as how bad must one need drugs? They really have lost all sense of morals and respect for their bodies. It is quite bloody sad, I never judge anyone as you never, ever know what one has experienced within their life. The night danced on and the brandy flowed within our bloodstreams and the cocaine travelled at light speed into our bodies. I had smoked endless menthol cigarettes, we sat on the doorstep outside of the hostel with our hazy minds, talking with slurred speech and bloodshot eyes.

We had been sat in his room towards the end of the night when he had said to me "Where d'ya think I could buy more coke?" I replied "I honestly have no clue mate, maybe ask someone outside the shop?" We had then walked round to the shop that was about thirty seconds around the corner from the hostel. He had spotted a group of people stood outside the corner shop then asked one of them "Excuse me mate? Do you where I could buy some coke?" It may seem strange to ask random people for coke but honestly we were in Fartown, anything goes round there.

I remember the person he had asked saying "Oh yeah I have some on me right now, do you want to buy it?" He then replied "Yeah go on then, how much?" The randomer gave him a price then we went back into the hostel and into his room. The guy I was with then said "Right Brandon, I will do a line first but if I start to overdose then flush it all down the toilet and ring an ambulance for me." I said in a very worried manner "Urm, yeah man of course! Are you sure you wanna take some though? I don't want you to die."

He then said "Yeah it is fine, I am choosing to do it but honestly ring an ambulance if anything happens to me." I just stood there waiting for him to do a line, hoping that he didn't drop dead in front of me. I remember being stood there feeling anxious as hell, I didn't want that on my head, I couldn't deal with the grief of somebody's death on my hands, especially if I were in the same room. He proceeded to put the coke into a line and then he snorted it. He was alright, he didn't overdose. Thank God for that!

I then did a line myself and we continued to drink the E&J. The night became morning, it was around 6:00 AM and the birds were tweeting and the sky was now a pale grey colour. It was officially morning, I remember feeling extremely worn out and woozy due to no sleep and the intoxicants within my body. I told the guy I was with "I am gonna get some sleep now mate, I am far gone." He then replied "Yeah me too pal, take care of yourself, I'll see you tomorrow." I wandered from his room to mine next door, I remember jumping onto my bed and instantly crashing out into sleep.

Oh am I glad that was all over, I was absolutely FUBAR. I remember this other time in that hostel in Fartown, I had been in the bathroom when I happened to look out of the bathroom window. I looked down at the back of the hostel and noticed there were a group of addicts stood in a circle. One of them had a needle in his hand, then proceeded to inject it into his neck, he was shooting up into a vein in his neck. I just looked down at them from this window in saddening shock. I couldn't imagine being like that, I don't judge them but honestly that is no way of living.

Poor souls man, I am purely grateful I am blessed in all the ways I am. I am so very glad that I do not do such things anymore as I hate the idea of getting messed up on drugs and drink now. I haven't touched anything like that in so long now, I can't even remember the last time I did any sort of substance. I am happy that I have no negative influences within my life now, no drugs or alcohol nor people of evil intent. I am free of all substances and evil-minded beings, I am truly and honestly away from all of that shite.

It is not good for anybody involved, I am just at peace knowing I did it all whilst I was young and stopped whilst I am young. I take extremely good care of myself now, I go to bed early and I eat healthily in this present time. I do everything a healthy person does,
I do not abuse myself no more, I am FREE from all torment and negativity. All my life, all I ever wanted was to be known by the world for my gifts and pain. All I want in my life is to be happy, healthy, successful and loved.

I have always dreamt of being a somebody, not just anybody. I am too gifted and I am too unique to just fall into the shadows. I haven't gone through all that pain, suffering and all those torturous memories for nothing. I was born to be a star, I was born to live for eternity through my work and inspiration. I want to be someone who helps and inspires others through my pain and mistakes. I am just praying that I will get there soon, I truly crave it. I have always wanted to be a successful artist, writer and even a little bit of a musician.

I just want my gifts to be seen and heard around the world. I pray to the universe that it all happens for me. It can't not happen, it really bloody needs to happen. I wasn't put here to just rot away and die a nobody. Forget that! I was put here to live for all eternity and shine forever like the stars in the night sky. I remember when I went to Geneva in Switzerland with my dad, back when I was around ten years old. I can't really remember much of that holiday as I was extremely young and was in Switzerland for around a week.

I remember getting a taxi from my dad's house all the way to the airport. I remember we were both sat in Manchester Airport eating fish and chips, looking out at all the departing planes. It was funny because I remember sitting there for about twenty minutes and my dad said "Bloody hell we need to go now, our plane is about to leave." My freshly made fish and chips were abandoned on the wooden table, I only had a few bites of my fish, then I had to leave it behind. We had flown over on an easyJet plane.

I remember looking out at the sky as I was sat by the window, it was so beautiful to see the landscape below me. I remember seeing the icicles collecting around the engine to my right. Me and my dad were sat next to an old man who asked me about my favourite football team but honestly I am not a football fan. I have never been into sport never mind football, my dad had bought a miniature bottle of Bell's whiskey and I got a Coca-Cola in a glass bottle. I remember the awfully strong scent of the whiskey lingering on my dad's breath.

We landed in Switzerland and I remember saying to my dad "Will everybody not understand what we are saying now that we are in Switzerland?" I was young and didn't think that there would be English-speaking people abroad! My dad replied to me "Of course they'll understand what we are saying, some of them won't and some of them will." We were picked up by my distant uncle in his silver BMW. It was pitch black as we had landed in Switzerland at night. My dad and I were staying with my aunt and uncle at their gorgeous villa-type house.

Me and my dad got to the house and were greeted by my aunt who is my dad's sister. I remember it looking like something from *Scarface*, it had a huge built-in pool in the garden, crystal white tiles and clear as snow water. The house had four floors and the carpet leading up the stairs was crimson red with a gold and white leaf pattern embedded into it. The stairs led up in a spiral motion, it was truly beautiful so be in such a wonderfully built house. I remember going down into the basement and seeing a World War Two bunker, it had a huge steel door that was impenetrable to the outside.

I asked my aunt "Why have you got a bunker in your home?" She replied "Oh that has been there since the Second World War, it was installed so that if the country was bombed or invaded people would be protected once inside it." My aunt showed me inside the bunker, it had these khaki green army camp beds and boxes of red wine dotted around the inside. I had never seen a bunker in real life before, it was quite eye opening to know that this could have been properly used during an invasion of the Nazis in the Second World War.

Switzerland was a safe haven for people fleeing nearby countries during the war as the Nazis didn't invade Switzerland and neither did the allies. It was a country that did not take sides which I suppose gave peace to those living in Switzerland and the civilians in the surrounding countries who fled when the bombs and soldiers landed on their soil. I have always truly loved Switzerland ever since I was there as a kid.

It has an invisible knot wrapped around my heart and each time I think of Switzerland it tugs a little more which draws me in every single time. I felt absolute peace within myself when I was over there, I felt like I was in my second home. Nobody knew me and I didn't know nobody. I felt a complete refresh on my soul and mind, I remember swimming in the pool every day I was over there. I would clean the pool for my aunt and uncle every night, the pool had built-in lights that lit up the inside of the pool which then illuminated the whole area surrounding the poolside. It looked so magical.

Me and my dad one day had played a pool game. We would take it in turns to drop a small-sized brick into the pool, then we would have to swim to the bottom of the pool and collect the brick without coming back up for air. I would whack my goggles on and swim all the way down to the bottom of the pool, collect the brick and then hand it to my dad. It was such a simple and fulfilling task that brought me such joy.

I remember one time I had just woken up in the morning. Every morning I would walk onto the balcony in my guest bedroom, then breathe in the morning air. I would take in the dream-like surroundings of the Swiss landscape. I looked down towards the poolside and that is when I noticed my cousins, who were Swiss, playing in the pool. They had come over to my aunt and uncle's house to see me and my dad. I got a bit freaked out to be honest because my cousin looked exactly like me but spoke no English and his complexion was a lot darker than mine. His hair was similar to mine and his features were so alike to mine that it made me feel like I was looking in the mirror at a foreign version of myself.

I quickly got changed into my swimming shorts, then bombed down the spiral stairs and into the garden. I tried to talk to my cousin but he had no idea what I was saying to him, I also didn't have a single clue what he was saying to me. I could see he was reading my lips to try and understand what I was saying but honestly it was like we were both aliens to one another. I remember speaking to him in a completely made-up language, I kept making sounds and saying random words to him but the words weren't real ones.

I bet he thought 'What the hell is he saying to me? Why is he making weird noises with his mouth?' Don't ask, I have no idea what I was doing, I was ten years old after all. Me and my cousin were playing in the pool with an inflatable crocodile and a homemade paddle. The homemade paddle was made from two square pieces of clear plastic which were then glued down onto a bamboo stick. The pieces of plastic were sharp on the corners which I didn't fully know about until I had thrown the paddle into the water.

I had ran from the grass next to the poolside and jumped into the crystal clear water, upon impact into the water I had landed on the paddle which then sliced a gash a few inches long into my left thigh. I remember shouting "Ow! I have just cut myself on the paddle!" I had immediately climbed out of the pool to look at my thigh. My aunt was a retired nurse so she knew exactly what to do, I remember her grabbing a medic kit and cleaning my wound with iodine, then putting a huge plaster over the wound.

It wasn't a deep cut or anything, it was more like a slice than a puncture wound. I still have the scar to this day and that happened over eleven years ago. I have always told people about how I got the scar as it is a constant reminder of when I were a kid, full of happiness in Switzerland. I look at the scar and it brings back many wonderful memories of when times were much, much different. I remember when me, my dad, my aunt and uncle had experienced a boat ride that sailed across a lake in Geneva.

It was truly heaven-like, I remember looking out into the distance and I could see the snowcapped Swiss Alps. I was on this boat surrounded by gorgeous sunlight but in the distance I could see the icy cold mountains of Switzerland. It was so strange to be enveloped in the hot climate but see snow in the distance. The Alps were massive, it was so delightful to experience the universe's wonders of nature. It is purely a masterpiece and a mystery as to how the universe has created such art like that landscape.

How nature is just here, for all to cherish and love. How nature will always be here for many years to come and then some. I find it euphoric that no man or woman could ever create such beauty. Nobody could envision the process of creating such amazingly beautiful landscapes. I remember when I was on this boat ride my dad had bought me a Swiss-style sandwich, it had cheese, a selection of meats, salad and a dressing that blanketed the whole of the contents.

I was only ten years old and didn't have a clue about what was in this sandwich and I know back then I didn't finish it, but my taste buds were completely different then as to how they are now. I would defo devour the sandwich now, I love cheese, salad and a variety of meats. It was like a continental sandwich but back then I didn't even know how to spell 'continental', never mind know what it meant. My dad had ended up eating the rest of it as I know it wasn't cheap and my dad doesn't like to waste his money, he can be very tightfisted. I ain't calling him out or anything, it is the truth.

I remember one night in Switzerland my aunt asked me "Do you want to try some of this chocolate milk drink?" Being a huge chocolate fan as a kid I quickly replied "Yes please, of course I would!" My aunt got this jar of chocolate powder out of the cupboard, but it wasn't like any other chocolate powder I had seen in England. It was to be drank either hot or cold, it was like Horlicks but chocolate flavoured. I remember drinking it cold with some full-fat milk and honestly the taste was like euphoria in liquid form.

I had downed the drink as though I had not drank fluid in days. I still can't remember the name of it but I know that it was truly lovely. Over here in England we have Nesquik but that Swiss drink tasted like gold compared to Nesquik. I remember when me and my dad had gone for a walk around the village by my aunt and uncle's house, we had stumbled upon a small, vintage looking shop. When we walked into the shop, a very lovely French woman had greeted us with "Bonjour, comment vas-tu?" I had learnt a little French in school but I only remembered that 'bonjour' means 'hello' and 'comment vas-tu?' means 'how are you?'

Me and my dad replied in our Yorkshire accents "Bonjour, are you okay?" I don't know why we went into this shop but my dad must have bought cigarettes or something because I don't remember getting anything. I loved how the people in Geneva spoke in their own languages. I heard French, German, Italian and Swiss accents lingering around the groups of people we passed in the streets. It is so beautiful to hear and see the mixed variety of cultures entwining with one another.

I seriously want to go back to Switzerland again in the near future so I can take my camera with me to capture many wonderful moments. I want to travel both in England and out of England, take my camera with me and snap many delightful images of people, places, food and sights that I surround myself with. I have always loved the idea of going around the world and meeting many great beings on my travels. One day I will go around the world with my camera, then create a photo album of all the sights, food, people and places I have experienced in the vast variety of cultures.

I have always said I want to, without being rude, sleep with women from different cultures and appreciate their heavenly beauty. Going from one side of the earth to another, then across another side, back over to somewhere else. Picking up the never ending memories of the universe around me. I am a big lover of food so I would definitely appreciate eating the selection of meals known to the countries I shall visit. I want to explore the universe around me and collect as much knowledge as possible to then add to my soul, mind and heart.

I want to see the world in all its beauty and delights. One thing I want to mention is that people are controlled by each other's perceptions on how to live their lives, the media is one big lie, well it can be at times. Who to believe? Social media is a machine built on fake mindsets and falsewords. Using the same sentences, same ideas and same styles. Nothing is original anymore, people are fake and would rather join the herd than create their own path within life. Dressing the same, eating the same, drinking the same, talking the same and doing the same as the person beside them.

Society is a brainwashing machine and people are the laundry, mixing together and always getting the same outcome, every time. They can't escape the patterns and paths of those around them that they must follow in order to feel like they truly matter. That is all a lie, we all must pave our own way through life and take what we see fit in order to benefit ourselves deeply and successfully, but doing it in a positive way. Their lives aren't their own, it is somebody else's that they have picked up, just like accidently opening the wrong washing machine door in a public laundry room.

They are all next to one another but because they all look the same from the outside, nobody can tell who is who without looking inside of them. That is how people are, from the outside they look the same but on the inside

I bet they don't even relate to those around them, it is all a front just to fit in and to not be left behind by the herd. YOU must create your own destiny so YOU can be fulfilled internally and externally.

Whose euphoria is that? I think I now know, its owner is quite lovely though. Full of joy like a vivid sunset, I watch her laugh, I cry hello. He gives his euphoria away, he loves the way she is. The only other sound is the rain outside, distant waves and birds awake. The woman is dream-like, love and deep. He now has his promises to keep, after sleepless nights and lots of sleep. Sweet dreams come to us as we lay, her and him rise from their bed, with thoughts of euphoria within their heads.

They stay inside away from the dread so they can get ready for the days ahead. I am completely brand new right now, I am not like my old ways in any way, shape or form. I do not do anything I used to do back in those hectic days. I am refreshed with all things golden, I am clean of all negative ways and things. I don't smoke, drink or do substances no more. I AM CLEAN OF ALL INTOXICANTS. My heart is pure, my soul is golden and my body is fresh. It is like I have done a factory reset on myself like you do with a mobile phone once you sell it to a shop.

I am completely brand new! I don't have any negativity in my body one bit, I am positive in all possible ways, I am refreshed in all my ways. I eat healthier now, I drink health-boosting fluids, I sleep over nine hours a night and I do regular walking each week. I am TOTALLY different now! NOBODY from my past will ever recognize this new Brandon as back then I was on a lower vibration, but now I am on a truly far higher vibration to those people. I am much, much different to everything and everyone within my past.

My past is dead and buried, long gone and forgotten. I am a new being now, I have the knowledge of many true things but I no longer carry the baggage of those negative ways. I have let go and remastered my life, self and soul. I am a golden soul, cleansed, healed, repaired and new in all possible ways. I am free from the shackles I once trailed around. I am free from all negative ways, I am free from all evil beings. I am something like a minimalist, I only have what I need.

I don't care for diamonds, clothes, cars or women. I only want one car, one bracelet, one necklace, one woman and one house. I want only a set of clothes I can wear each week and a pair of shoes that I can wear every day that are comfy and do the job they were designed for. All of those materialistic items that many people claim they need can be destroyed, burnt, lost and stolen. What can't be lost, destroyed, stolen or burnt is our knowledge and our souls.

As long as we have our health, happiness, love, success, warmth, shelter, food and family then we have all that we possibly need, every other thing that we want in our lives is a gift and not a necessity. Materials can be destroyed in an instant but we can get them back once we buy them again. Yes I know we need money to live in this world, I am not saying that money is bad, of course money is an excellent thing and can be a great tool in one's life.

Money allows us to live in the way we see fit but money can also change those around us and can definitely change ourselves if we aren't grounded enough. I love money but I don't let it warp my mind and take over my life. I use it as a tool of bettering myself and those around me. I am at peace with my life and self, I am content with all that I have as I know that there is somebody out there in the world who has nothing at all. They are praying for the things I have so if I were to be ungrateful of those things, it is basically showing the universe that I don't care for what I have and that none of it matters.

WE must show gratitude for the things WE do have

not the things WE don't as there is always somebody happier with less than US. Less is sometimes more and more is sometimes less, WE must decide what we need and what we don't need in order to achieve inner contentment. WE must show ourselves that WE can be happier with less as just because WE might have more doesn't mean that WE will be happy, it is an illusion that WE think by having more means WE will feel more.

Happiness, health and love doesn't measure into money and materialism, money and materialism cannot buy you a lover, it cannot buy you a new body and it cannot buy you happiness once you are depressed. Yes money is great for many beautiful reasons but please do not let materialism and money be the only driving force within your life. Once your health is lost it cannot be gained but if your money-packed wallet was lost you know that the money can be made back and you will still have your health.

Choose what truly matters because we often fill our lives with pointless materialistic things that do not help us grow and do not show us our true potential. When we overfill our lives with pointless belongings we become drowned in vanity and egotistical matters. We always look to try and impress others by what we have instead of trying to show others what we are inside. What truly makes a person is their hearts, minds and souls, not what they own or how much money they have. People will remember you for how you were, not what you had.

WE all must think about life in a different light so WE can all grow together as a society. Every other material item can be destroyed and created again, those things I listed before cannot be created again once lost. We must care for the things that truly matter and make us better people each and every day. I have my own style, my own mind and my own means. I do not need outside validation from anybody, none of us do.

We only need the validation of ourselves. All outside sources are merely a set of passing comments that can't affect us unless we let them. I only wear simple and comfy clothing that is inexpensive. I am not materialistic in anyway shape or form, I like to have what I need and some things of what I desire, I mean we all have those certain desires but we must control them before they control us. I do not crave fame nor do I crave fortune, I do not want a flashy car or an over-the-top house, I just want love, happiness, health, family and a girl who truly loves me.

I just want a minimal lifestyle, a simple life with simple things. I do not need to show off nor do I want to. The universe will always deliver to me all that I need, I do not want a lot at all. I believe we are living in an extremely terrible consumerist-ridden life. It is all about status and how much money you have, how many cars you have and how many houses you own. I don't care for what others think or feel about me. I know what I know of myself and my life, that is all that matters.

The important things in life are food and drink, health, happiness, love, success, warmth, shelter and family. As long as we have clothes on our backs, shoes on our feet and all of the above, that is what truly matters. We do not need over-consumption as this will only lead to unhappiness and ill-health. I don't really care for social media. It is the simple things in life that bring us the most joy and happiness. My mother always used to say and still does say that "Without your health you have nothing."

It is so true, I have experienced life without full health and honestly I had nothing I was happy about as my mind was not in a good place. So because of having poor mental health, the rest of my life was ill as well. I only care for what I need, what brings me happiness, health, love and contentment. I have had many things within my past and truly I have lost it all then gained it all

205

back but now I see that none of that could have ever solved my previous illnesses I have endured. Life is the greatest gift of all.

I AM FREE FROM ALL WICKEDNESS AND NEGATIVITY IN ALL THEIR WAYS. I AM PURE AND FLOWING WITH THE UNIVERSE. I AM HEALED, RESTORED AND CLEANSED INSIDE AND OUT! I NO LONGER HOLD ONTO ANY BADNESS. I AM PURELY FREE AND GOLDEN. I LOVE MY LIFE, MYSELF AND THE UNIVERSE INSIDE AND OUT. I encourage everyone reading this to get the help you want and need in order to be successfully complete and happy with your lives inside and out, just like I am.

I just want to say that I forgive everybody who has ever hurt or harmed me within my life, you have all taught me valuable lessons that have shaped me into the resilient person I now am. I even forgive Lauren for the pain she caused me as all of that pain has now been turned into success. You have read about my life and struggles and now you have read that I am pure and free from all past torment, wickedness and negativity.

YOU can do it just like I have, so please take all of this into consideration and use my pain as a guiding light to free yourself from any sort of negative destruction. YOU can do it! I believe in you my friend. Honestly use my words and my experiences to battle on through the pain and trust me you will also live an abundantly happy, healthy and successful life. YOU can push through it my friend. I believe you have the power within to do anything you desire. YOU are wonderful, beautiful and golden my friend.

Trust in your inner self and the universe, you will get where you want and need to be. YOU must trust in the universe and yourself in order to successfully claim VICTORY in your life. YOU can defeat the demons that torment you, I have and honestly once you do, YOU WILL BE CONTENT! I no longer worry, stress or am in pain anymore. I AM FREE! YOU also can be FREE my friend! KEEP YOUR HEAD HELD HIGH, KEEP THE FIRE INSIDE OF YOU AND BANISH THE DEMONS THAT TRY TO HARM YOU.

I believe in you my friend! YOU can be successful in all of your beautiful ways and means. YOU CAN DO IT! YOU WILL SUCCEED AND YOU WILL LIVE TO TELL THE TALE! Just like how I have done in my own life. YOU MUST WIN AGAINST THE SUFFERING. I KNOW YOU CAN DO IT MY FRIEND! WE CAN ALL BE HAPPY, HEALTHY, SUCCESSFUL AND LOVED TOGETHER. CHANGE YOUR MINDSET AND YOU WILL LIVE A EUPHORICALLY LOVELY LIFE. I want to finish and just say that I do believe I am truly gifted, not mentally unwell.

I honestly believe that I have only had many dark nights of my soul, not that I am mentally unwell. I AM GIFTED NOT MENTALLY UNSTABLE. In life we are given many labels for ourselves and for life in general. I am just gifted not insane, I see and feel things differently to others, I have natural gifts that have been given to me by the lovely universe. I am blessed with a wonderful variety of gifts, I am not mentally unwell like the doctor's notes say, they will think anyone is unwell just because they see the light in life and speak of truths that nobody else dares to speak.

Like I said, I am gifted, not unwell. Oh think of how many other gifted souls remain locked away in isolation in the corridors of hospitals knowing they are gifted but the doctors say otherwise. The doctors will label you sick when you see the truth behind life, when you connect with the universe and spirit world. Not all people can do such things but because of this they label us mad. We gifted ones aren't mad, we are blessed, chosen by the ones above, the ones who see and know all, THE UNIVERSE.

I feel like I am a lot older than my actual age, I may be twenty-two but I feel like I have wandered this earth many lifetimes before this one. I have always felt extremely different to others around me, always felt like I can see and feel things much deeper and more articulately than others. I have always said that I was born in the wrong era, like I would have enjoyed a life of someone who lived hundreds of years ago. I love my life now and everything within it, I wouldn't change anything in my life right now but I have always had this strange feeling like I am not home, like I am not living in my proper home.

I feel like my home is elsewhere, far, far away from this dimension. I know that I am not meant to live where I do now for all my life, I am meant for somewhere else, somewhere where it is closer to my real, true home. Don't get me wrong, I appreciate all that I have now but I can't help but feel disconnected from this realm. I will be guided by the divine towards my true path, I am guided and loved by the spirits of the divine, I know that they are with me all the time and will make sure I get to where I am supposed to be.

I am a believer in the spirit world and the afterlife. I believe we all have spirit guides around us, we all have angels around us to protect and help us in times of need. I know that we are merely flesh and bone in this world but once we die our souls are reunited with our loved ones who have passed and we will all live back in our actual homes. Our homes in the spirit world where everything is warm, bright and euphorically dream-like. I am not afraid of death as I know that my pain, whatever it be, shall be over and my soul can go home to where it is truly at peace.

I am content in knowing that life doesn't end in death, it is just the death of my physical self not my actual self. My soul shall live for all eternity in many different lifetimes and bodies. My soul will live for all eternity within all these words and I will live in the hearts and minds of those who have read this book, for all eternity. Thank you for reading this book, it truly means the world to me that you have taken the time out of your life to read it. I share with you my love and light, you are a wonderful person and I hope that I have helped you in one way or another by publishing this book.

I want to inspire YOU to be the person YOU want to be and to be free from all the demons that try bring you down. YOU have the courage and light within YOU to live the life YOU desire my friend. I believe in YOU!